"Antony and McCabe have presented evidence-based treatments for panic disorder from both psychological and pharmacological view points in a superbly clear and succinct manner. Undoubtedly, their overview will be a tremendous aid for individuals in need of treatment guidance for panic disorder. Their review provides an excellent resource for professionals as well."

—Michelle G. Craske, Ph.D.,
professor of psychology, University
of California, Los Angeles

D0616126

10 Simple Solutions to Panic

How to Overcome Panic Attacks,
Calm Physical Symptoms
& Reclaim Your Life

MARTIN M. ANTONY, PH.D.
RANDI E. M^cCABE, PH.D.

New Harbinger Publications, Inc.

This book is dedicated to all of our patients and clients, whose courage and perseverance have taught us most about overcoming anxiety.

—Martin M. Antony
—Randi E. McCabe

Publisher's Note

Distributed in Canada by Raincoast Books

Copyright © 2004 by Martin Antony and Randi McCabe
New Harbinger Publications, Inc.
5674 Shattuck Avenue
Oakland, CA 94609

Cover design by Amy Shoup
Text design by Michele Waters-Kermes

ISBN-10 1-57224-325-2
ISBN-13 978-1-57224-325-5

Printed in the United States of America

New Harbinger Publications' website address: www.newharbinger.com

10   09   08

10 9 8 7 6 5 4 3

Contents

Acknowledgments

We would like to thank Sam Katerji for her assistance in preparing this book. We are also grateful to our editors at New Harbinger, Catharine Sutker and Carole Honeychurch, for their support and careful attention to detail. Finally, a special thanks to the many individuals who are responsible for originally developing and studying the treatments described in this book, including James Ballenger, David H. Barlow, Aaron T. Beck, David M. Clark, Michele G. Craske, Donald F. Klein, Isaac Marks, S. Rachman, Ron Rapee, and many others.

Introduction

About a third of people report having panic attacks from time to time (Norton, Dorward, and Cox 1986), and increasingly, panic attacks are becoming recognized as a common experience. Although the term "panic attack" was not officially used until the early 1980s (American Psychiatric Association 1980), it is now a familiar phrase in our culture. The topic appears frequently in the media, and a number of celebrities, including Donny Osmond, Kim Basinger, and Willard Scott, have spoken openly about their struggles with panic. In fact, one of the "frequently asked questions" listed on the Web site www.healthypet.com is "What can I do about my dog's panic attacks?" That's right—it seems that even dogs may have panic attacks!

Essentially, a panic attack is a rush of fear involving intense physical sensations, and for most people, panic attacks are triggered by particular feared situations. For example, people who experience anxiety over presentations may have a panic attack when giving a speech. Likewise, people who fear heights often experience panic attacks in high places. For the most part, this book will not discuss panic attacks that are triggered by commonly feared objects and situations such as these. Instead, the emphasis of this book is on panic attacks that occur unexpectedly or "out of the blue" in a condition known as *panic disorder.*

Panic disorder is an anxiety disorder in which individuals experience panic attacks that are not associated with any obvious trigger or cause. The attacks can occur at any time or in any place, including during times of relaxation or when lying in bed, fast asleep. Often they occur in public places or in situations from which escape is difficult (e.g., a movie theater or crowded bus). Because panic is typically accompanied by frightening symptoms such as racing heart, sweating, dizziness, and feelings of unreality, the attacks may be mistaken as signs of a heart attack, stroke, fainting, or an impending loss of control (for instance, going crazy or not making it to the bathroom in time). However, despite these fears, panic attacks are generally not at all dangerous.

Is this Book for You?

This book is likely to be useful if you answer "yes" to most of the following questions:

- Do you experience intense periods of fear that begin quickly and that are accompanied by several uncomfortable physical symptoms, such as racing heart, nausea, breathlessness, and dizziness?

- Do these periods of fear appear to occur out of the blue, even in situations where you don't expect to feel anxious or nervous?

- Do you anticipate the attacks, wondering when the next one will strike?

- Do you worry about the possible consequences of the attacks? For example, during the attacks do you worry that you might die, faint, go crazy, lose control, vomit, lose bowel control, have a stroke, or embarrass yourself?

- Do you fear or avoid situations where the attacks often occur? Are there other things that you do to protect yourself from experiencing panic attacks?

- Do your panic attacks and the tendency to avoid feared situations interfere with your life? For example, does the problem affect your work, hobbies, or relationships?

- Are you ready to work on your panic attacks? If you are too busy, or if there are other problems that are likely to get in the way (for example, severe depression or significant alcohol or drug use), this may not be the best time to begin working on your panic.

Can a Self-Help Book Really Help?

There are a number of reasons to assume that a book such as this one may be helpful. First, the strategies described in this book have been researched extensively, and there are a lot of studies showing that these treatments are effective when administered by a trained therapist (Antony and Swinson 2000). In addition, there is quite a bit of evidence that the strategies described in this book are effective for many people even when administered in a self-help format (Gould and Clum 1995; Hecker, Losee, Fritzler, and Fink 1996). Of course, simply *reading* this book will not make your panic attacks go away, any more than just reading a book on physical fitness will help you to get in shape. To get the most out of it, you will need to practice the strategies described in the book over and over again.

Researchers have shown that self-help treatments often work better when they are accompanied by occasional visits to a doctor or therapist to discuss your progress (Febbraro, Clum, Roodman, and Wright 1999). If you find it difficult to use the strategies in this book on your own, you may want to consider combining the treatments described with occasional visits to a professional therapist or to a family doctor who is experienced with treating panic disorder.

This book is designed for people who are interested in knowing the basics about how to overcome problems with panic, but who don't necessarily want to read a larger book on the topic. If you find, after reading this book, that you want to learn more, there are a number of other excellent books on overcoming panic. Some of our favorites are listed in the recommended readings section at the back of this book. You may also benefit from obtaining additional treatment via the Internet (one excellent site can be found at: www.paniccenter.net), by joining a support group in your community, or by seeking help with a professional therapist.

If you do seek professional help, we highly recommend that you make sure the individual is experienced in treating panic disorder, either with medications or with cognitive behavioral therapy. As discussed throughout this book, these are the two main treatments that have been found to be effective for this problem. A couple of good sources of information on professionals who treat this problem include the Anxiety Disorders Association of America (www.adaa.org) and the Anxiety Disorders Association of Canada (www.anxietycanada.ca).

Don't be fooled by the size of this book. Though you may be able to read it in one sitting, your panic attacks will not go away overnight. The strategies described here are meant to be used almost daily over an extended period of time. It will also be important to monitor your progress carefully. A journal or notebook will be the one essential tool you'll need to work through the all the exercises in this book. Many of the techniques described here require you to take notes, to record your experiences, and to monitor your use of various treatment strategies. Exercises requiring the journal begin early on, so you may want to have it handy before you start reading chapter 1. With a bit of luck and lots of hard work, you should notice a significant decrease in anxiety after using the strategies for a number of weeks or months.

Fortunately, panic disorder is among the most treatable of psychological problems. The strategies described in this book have been researched extensively and have consistently been shown to be effective for combating panic attacks and related anxiety problems. If you put your mind to it, you *can* feel better.

Understand Your Panic and Fear

The purpose of this introductory chapter is to set the stage for overcoming your difficulties with panic. To start, it's important to understand exactly what a panic attack is and what is meant by other relevant terms, including "anxiety," "panic disorder," and "agoraphobia." In addition to providing the definitions of these terms, this chapter will also provide important background information regarding the nature of, causes, and proven treatments for panic attacks and panic disorder.

Defining Fear and Anxiety

In everyday life, terms such as "fear," "anxiety," "worry," and "panic" are often used interchangeably. However, for the purpose of understanding the nature of these problems, we will distinguish between these terms. We begin with definitions of fear and anxiety.

Fear is a basic emotion that is experienced by all people. It is a reaction to an immediate danger (or at least an immediate *perceived* danger), and it is sometimes referred to as a "fight or flight" response. This is because when people experience fear, their physical and mental resources are focused on protecting the self from the threat, either by fleeing from the situation or by defending themselves with an aggressive response toward whoever or whatever is producing the threat.

When we feel fear, our bodies become activated. Our hearts race to ensure that oxygen-rich blood is circulated to the areas of the body that need it. We breathe more heavily to provide the extra oxygen that's required to facilitate escape. We also sweat, which cools off the body so it can perform more effectively. In addition to the physical changes that occur during fear, there are also cognitive changes (the term "cognition" simply means "thought"). We tend to focus almost exclusively on the source of the threat, which makes it difficult to think about other things, including whatever you happen to be doing at the time. Fear is also accompanied by a strong urge to do almost anything to get rid of the feeling, such as escape from the situation.

Anxiety is related to the emotion of fear, but there are important differences between anxiety and fear. Anxiety tends to be more future-oriented. Whereas fear is a reaction to an immediate threat (like being attacked by a dog), anxiety occurs when we anticipate a future threat of some kind (like worrying about an upcoming exam). Compared to fear, anxiety tends to be more diffuse, harder to describe, longer lasting, and slower to come on. When we feel anxious, we may experience some of the same physical symptoms that occur during fear (for instance, nausea, dizziness), but other common features of anxiety include muscle tension, sleeplessness, and worry about future events.

What Is a Panic Attack?

As we mentioned in the introduction, a panic attack is a rush of fear. It is an immediate response to a perceived threat, and it is accompanied by intense physical sensations. According to the official definition (American Psychiatric Association 2000), a panic attack must include at least four of the following thirteen symptoms:

1. Racing or pounding heart
2. Sweating
3. Trembling or shaking
4. Shortness of breath
5. Feeling of choking
6. Chest pain or discomfort
7. Nausea or abdominal distress
8. Feeling dizzy, unsteady, or faint
9. Feeling unreal or detached
10. Numbness or tingling sensations
11. Chills or hot flushes
12. Fear of dying
13. Fear of going crazy or losing control

In addition to these defining symptoms, it is not unusual for people to experience other uncomfortable feelings, including blurred vision or a tight feeling in the throat. Panic attacks tend to increase in intensity very quickly, often reaching their peak within seconds (though according to the official definition, the peak can be reached within ten minutes or less). The attacks typically last anywhere from a few minutes to an hour or so. Although some people report "panic attacks" lasting many hours or days, these are probably not true attacks. Instead, such individuals are likely experiencing multiple panic attacks throughout the day, with high levels of anxiety in between.

What is Panic Disorder?

Panic disorder is an anxiety disorder in which individuals experience panic attacks out of the blue, without any obvious trigger or cause. In some cases, attacks are relatively infrequent (perhaps once every few months), but they can also occur as frequently as many times per day. In addition, people with panic disorder are frightened by their attacks. They worry about when the next attack will occur, and they worry about the possible consequences of the attacks (for example, whether they will die, lose control, go crazy, vomit, have diarrhea, or faint). They also change their behavior in order to cope with the attacks or to prevent them from occurring altogether. The development of agoraphobic avoidance (to be defined shortly) is the most common type of behavioral change that occurs in panic disorder, though there may be other types of behavioral changes as well. Some examples include:

- Carrying medication, money, cellular telephone, pager, water, or other safety items
- Avoiding activities (like exercise or sex) that trigger panic-like symptoms of physical arousal
- Insisting on being accompanied when leaving the house
- Drinking alcohol to combat feelings of panic
- Avoiding caffeine, alcohol, or other substances
- Frequently checking your pulse or blood pressure
- Distracting yourself from the symptoms (for instance, reading a book on the subway)
- Always needing to know where your spouse or partner is

- Sitting near exits when at the movies or at a restaurant

Before a diagnosis of panic disorder can be given, it is important to rule out any medical conditions or possible substance-related reasons for the attacks. Examples of medical disorders that can trigger symptoms of anxiety and panic include thyroid problems, balance disorders, seizure disorders, and cardiac conditions. Use of stimulants (like cocaine, caffeine, diet pills, and certain other medications), withdrawal from alcohol, and use of other drugs (like marijuana) can also trigger panic-like feelings. Before assuming that your symptoms are due to an anxiety disorder, it's important to have a full medical workup to determine whether there is a physical cause for your problems. Once physical causes are ruled out, you can be much more confident when trying the strategies described in this book.

What Is Agoraphobia?

Most people with panic disorder develop some degree of agoraphobia. The term agoraphobia is often misunderstood. Some people mistakenly believe that it's a fear of open spaces. Others assume that this problem is a fear of leaving the home. Although a small percentage of people with agoraphobia may fear open spaces, a fear of open spaces is actually quite uncommon among people who suffer from this condition. Furthermore, only the most severe forms of agoraphobia are associated with an inability to leave one's house.

Agoraphobia is a fear of situations in which escape might be difficult or in which help might not be available in the event of experiencing a panic attack or panic-like symptoms (the literal translation of agoraphobia is "a fear of the market place"). The types of situations that people with agoraphobia avoid include:

- Crowded places: Supermarkets, theaters, malls, sports events

- Enclosed places, and places from which escape is difficult: Tunnels, small rooms, elevators, airplanes, subways, buses, getting a haircut, long lines

- Driving: Especially on highways and bridges, in bad traffic, and over long distances. Being a passenger in a car may also be difficult.

- Being away from home: Some individuals have a safe distance around their home and find it difficult to travel beyond that distance. In rare cases, leaving the home may be completely impossible.

- Being alone: Especially in the situations listed above

For some people, agoraphobia is very mild (for example, just a fear of panicking on overseas flights), or there may be no agoraphobic avoidance at all. For others, agoraphobia can be very severe, preventing the individual from doing just about anything outside the home. For most people who suffer from panic disorder, the level of agoraphobic avoidance is somewhere in between these two extremes.

Facts about Panic Disorder and Agoraphobia

In this section, we provide a few facts about panic disorder that may be of interest. Full reviews on these topics are available elsewhere (for example, Antony and Swinson 2000; Taylor 2000). Panic disorder is a relatively common condition, affecting about 3.5 percent of the general population at some time in their lives (Kessler et al. 1994). If you do the math, that's more than ten million Americans. About two thirds of people with panic disorder are women. In addition, women with panic disorder are more likely than men with panic disorder to have more frequent panic attacks, more severe agoraphobia, and a more intense fear of panic symptoms (Turgeon, Marchand, and Dupuis 1998).

Panic disorder tends to begin in early adulthood (during a person's 20s), though it can also begin in childhood or late in life. The onset of panic disorder is usually somewhat sudden, often beginning with a bad panic attack. Also, the onset often follows a period of stress in a person's life, including events such as graduation, divorce, a new marriage, a new baby, a new job, unemployment, death of a loved one, or illness in the family (for a review, see Antony and Swinson 2000).

Without treatment, panic disorder tends to be a chronic problem. For example, one study found that 92 percent of individuals with panic disorder were still experiencing panic attacks a year after their initial assessment (Ehlers 1995). The good news is that panic disorder is a very treatable condition—a point we will return to later in this chapter.

Panic disorder affects a wide range of life domains including work, recreation, and social functioning. In fact, a study from our clinic (Antony, Roth, Swinson, Huta, and Devins 1998) found levels of impairment in functioning among people with panic disorder to be similar to impairment levels of people with serious medical conditions, such as kidney disease and multiple sclerosis. If you suffer from panic disorder, this finding may not be all that surprising to you. Panic disorder is also costly in terms of its impact on the health-care system and on society in general. For example, Siegel, Jones, and Wilson (1990) found that people with panic disorder visit physicians seven times more often than people without panic disorder, and they miss twice as many work days.

Findings from our clinic (Antony and Swinson 2000) confirm those from a number of other centers showing that panic disorder often occurs along with other problems. For example, we found that almost one out of five individuals seeking treatment for panic disorder at our center also suffered from depression. Almost a quarter had significant problems with anxiety in social situations, and many individuals had other types of anxiety disorders, including phobias, generalized anxiety disorder, and obsessive compulsive disorder. Fortunately, the presence of another anxiety disorder or depression often doesn't have an impact on the outcome of treatment for panic disorder. In fact, targeting the panic disorder can lead to improvements in the other problems as well (Brown, Antony, and Barlow 1995).

Exercise: Understanding Your Problems with Panic

In the previous section we reviewed some of the typical patterns often seen in people with panic disorder. How does your own experience match what has been found in the research? In your journal, record your responses to the questions below. Think about how your own experiences compare to the "average" person who participates in research studies on panic disorder.

- How old were you when you experienced your first panic attack?

- Were you experiencing any life stress during the year before your panic attacks began? If so, what types of stresses?

- What areas of your life are most affected by your panic attacks (work/school, social functioning, leisure)?

- In addition to your panic attacks, do you experience other problems with anxiety, depression, excessive alcohol or drug use, or other difficulties?

Causes of Panic Disorder and Agoraphobia

The causes of panic disorder are complex, and there is no single factor that is responsible for the problem in all cases. Furthermore, it's impossible to determine the specific cause of the disorder for any single individual. The best we can do, based on the current state of the research, is discuss the types of factors that are believed to play a role in the development of panic disorder, based on studies of large groups of individuals who suffer from the problem. Whether the results of these studies are relevant to your own case is impossible to know. So, if you read somewhere that panic disorder is caused by a chemical imbalance in the brain, bad genes, or bad parenting, don't believe everything you read. These factors may play a role for some individuals, but they are only part of the story.

Perhaps the best way to think about the cause of your own problems with panic is to understand that in all likelihood the problem has come about through a complex interaction between psychological factors (your learning history, beliefs, etc.), biological factors (genetic vulnerabilities), and environmental factors (like stress). Although it is not necessary to completely understand what causes panic disorder to be able to overcome it, recognizing the ways in which various factors influence the course of the problem can be enlightening.

BIOLOGICAL FACTORS

Over the past twenty years, much evidence has been accumulated to support the view that our biology influences whether we develop problems with panic attacks and panic disorder, as well as the course that these problems can take over time. First, there are numerous studies showing that panic disorder is influenced by genetic factors. For example, relatives of people with panic disorder are three times as likely to develop the problem than are relatives of people without panic disorder (Mannuzza, Chapman, Klein, and Fyer 1994, 1995). Furthermore, researchers have found that genetics is at least partially responsible for the transmission of panic disorder from generation to generation, though environmental factors (like learning) also play a role (Kendler et al. 1992, 1993).

In addition, there is considerable evidence that certain neurotransmitters in the brain play a role in panic disorder. Neurotransmitters are chemicals that transmit information from one nerve cell to another. The ones that seem to be most involved in panic disorder are noreprinephrine, serotonin, and cholecystokinin (for a review, see Antony and Swinson 2000). For example, substances that increase levels of norepinephrine in the brain can trigger panic attacks. In addition, the medications that are most effective for treating panic disorder (see chapter 10 for a review) work by affecting either serotonin or norepinephrine activity.

Finally, there is evidence that certain areas of the brain are particularly active among people with panic disorder, especially during panic attacks. One such area is the parahippocampal region, located on the right side of the brain. Studies looking at blood flow in the brain have found increased activity in this area among people experiencing fear or panic. However, it's difficult to form any definite conclusions about the role of the brain in panic disorder because studies often find conflicting results (see Antony and Swinson 2000).

PSYCHOLOGICAL FACTORS

Perhaps the most influential psychological theory to explain the process of panic was developed by the British psychologist David M. Clark (1986, 1988). According to Clark, people have unexpected panic attacks because they catastrophically misinterpret the meaning of physical sensations that, in reality, are perfectly safe. Just as believing that dogs are dangerous can lead to panic and fear in the presence of dogs, believing that physical symptoms such as racing heart, dizziness, and breathlessness are dangerous can lead to panic and fear whenever these symptoms are experienced. And of course, we all experience these symptoms from time to time for reasons that are not at all dangerous. If you are afraid of these symptoms, or if you interpret them as a sign of danger, it makes sense that you would react with panic when they occur.

There is lots of research supporting this view of panic disorder. As reviewed by Antony and Swinson (2000), people with panic disorder tend to pay attention to panic-related information, are very aware of panic-related symptoms, and are very fearful of these symptoms when they occur. Compared to people without panic disorder, individuals with panic disorder are more likely to interpret ambiguous physical symptoms as a sign of immediate danger, and they tend to believe these interpretations more strongly (Clark et al. 1997; Harvey, Richards, Dziadosz, and Swindell 1993). The types of physical symptoms that people experience during their panic attacks are closely linked to the types of thoughts that they have (Marks et al. 1991). For example, sensations such as racing heart, shortness of breath, and numbness and tingling are often interpreted as a sign of impending physical disaster (like a heart attack) by people with panic disorder. In contrast, feelings of depersonalization are more likely to be interpreted as a sign of some sort of psychological disaster (like losing control or going crazy).

Of course, in reality, these are all perfectly normal symptoms that people experience when they are frightened, and often they are not a sign of any catastrophe whatsoever. As you will see in the next section, teaching people to change their anxious beliefs about panic and the physical sensations they experience is a powerful way to prevent panic attacks in the future.

Effective Treatments for Panic Disorder

Just as both biological and psychological factors contribute to the development and maintenance of panic disorder over time, both biological and psychological treatments have been shown to be effective for treating this condition. The outcome of these treatments depends on the individual. A small percentage of people get no benefit from treatment, and some get only partial benefit. For most people, however, treatment leads to significant gains, and up to half of individuals are almost completely free of panic symptoms by the end of treatment. In addition, certain herbal remedies and lifestyle changes (like getting regular exercise) may help. Each of these approaches is discussed in detail through this book, so we will provide only a brief overview here.

With respect to biological treatments, the most commonly used approaches include anti-anxiety medications (like alprazolam, clonazepam) and certain antidepressants, including the selective serotonin reuptake inhibitors (for instance, fluoxetine, paroxetine) and tricyclic antidepressants (like imipramine). Note that although these drugs are called antidepressants, they are effective for reducing anxiety and panic attacks regardless of whether an individual experiences depression.

The only form of psychological treatment that has consistently been shown in controlled studies to be effective for treating panic disorder is cognitive behavioral therapy or CBT. Treatment usually lasts ten to fifteen weeks, and includes a combination of strategies from the following list:

EDUCATION. The information about the nature of panic attacks and panic disorder that makes up this component of treatment is similar to the information you are learning in this chapter.

COGNITIVE RESTRUCTURING. This strategy involves teaching people to become more aware of their anxious beliefs and to examine the evidence regarding those beliefs. The goal of cognitive restructuring is to shift anxious patterns of thinking to more balanced, realistic thinking based on a thorough consideration of all the evidence (instead of focusing only on the evidence that supports your anxious thoughts). You'll learn how to do cognitive restructuring in chapter 4.

EXPOSURE TO FEARED SITUATIONS. One of the most powerful ways to overcome fear is by confronting the feared situation head on. Exposure to feared agoraphobic situations (like driving, being in crowds, or being alone) is a very effective way to overcome a fear of being in these situations. You'll learn about situational exposure in chapter 5.

EXPOSURE TO FEARED SENSATIONS. Because people with panic disorder are fearful of experiencing panic sensations such as dizziness and breathlessness, treatment often includes repeated exposure to feared sensations (for example, spinning in a chair to get dizzy) until they no longer arouse fear. This type of exposure is called *interoceptive exposure* or *symptom exposure,* and you'll learn how to use it in chapter 6.

BREATHING RETRAINING. As you will learn in chapter 8, breathing too quickly for the body's needs (also called *hyperventilation*) can trigger symptoms of panic. Learning to slow down your breathing using a technique called "breathing retraining" may help to prevent symptoms that are worsened by hyperventilating during panic attacks.

You may be wondering, what works better, CBT, medication, or a combination of these approaches. In most studies comparing these three options, all three work about equally well in the short term, on average. In other words, over the course of treatment (usually a few months), the same percentage of people tend to respond to CBT, medication, or combined treatment (for a review, see Antony and Swinson 2000).

However, that doesn't mean that these approaches are equally likely to work for *you* or for any other specific individual. Some people who don't respond to CBT still do well with medication (Hoffart et al. 1993), and some people who don't respond to medication still benefit from CBT (Pollack et al. 1994). Furthermore, some people seem to respond best to the combination of these approaches. Unfortunately, there is no proven way to predict who is going to respond best to one approach versus another except trial and error.

Even though medication, CBT, and combined treatments work equally well in the short term, the more important question is what works best in the long term. There are at least two large studies (Barlow, Gorman, Shear, and Woods 2000; Marks et al. 1993) showing that in the long term, CBT is probably a better option for most people. The problem with medication is a higher rate of relapse upon trying to discontinue the treatment. A larger percentage of people who take medication relapse during the years following treatment than is the case with CBT, for which treatment gains tend to be maintained over time. Also, for people who receive both medication and CBT, one predictor of long-term outcome is their beliefs regarding why they improved. In a study on combined behavior therapy and medication, Başoğlu et al. (1994) found that those who believed it was the medication that led to their improvement were more likely to worsen during the six months following the end of treatment than were those who believed it was the behavior therapy (and thus their own efforts) that led to their gains.

Make a Contract and Set Realistic Goals

Now that you have a better understanding of your panic attacks and anxiety, the next step is to begin planning to conquer your fears. Treatment for panic involves a number of steps:

- Monitoring your panic symptoms so you can learn about your own patterns of responding and identify situations or triggers that make you feel vulnerable

- Learning new strategies to manage your panic symptoms so you're no longer fearful of intense physical sensations

- Developing your skills at identifying and counteracting anxious thoughts

- Gradually confronting the triggers, physical sensations, or situations that make you feel anxious and panicky

- Reducing your avoidance and use of safety behaviors (for example, carrying certain items such as a cell phone, water, or medication, or being accompanied by a familiar person)

As you follow the steps in this book, you will find that your anxiety and avoidance are reduced and your sense of confidence is restored. You will begin to regain your life and your comfort level will begin to improve, perhaps even returning to where it was before you first experienced panic. You will no longer feel as if you must always confine yourself to a "safe zone."

The treatment steps that you will follow throughout this book require effort on your part. If you want to feel better, you'll need to practice the strategies that you learn on a daily basis. The strategies will not be useful if you just learn them passively, and they will not be effective if you just read them without implementing them in your life. We'll be asking you to write your experiences down so that you can examine and learn from them. You will need to have the courage to gradually challenge your fears. Ideally, you will set aside some time each day to devote to overcoming your panic. As you can see, these steps require commitment from you. Commitment will involve time, mental resources, and emotional energy. But by making this investment, your life will change for the better.

Make a Commitment to Change

It may be hard to find the time to learn and practice the material in this book. You may have a very busy life and may find it hard to have an extra minute in your day to focus on yourself. Following through with these solutions will require you to *make* the time by prioritizing and by scheduling time each day for yourself and your well being. When you think about how much of your time has been spent consumed by your anxiety and fear of panic symptoms, it may be worth it for you to set aside time in the next couple of months to conquer your anxiety and take back your life.

Exercise: Planning for Treatment

Take some time now to examine how you are going to make change a priority. On a new page in your journal, provide answers to the following questions:

- How will you reorganize your life to set aside time for yourself to practice the strategies you learn as you work through the following chapters?

- What other commitments may interfere with following through with your plan? What solutions can you use to manage these other commitments?

- What are your motivations for overcoming your panic?

- How will your life change once you are no longer controlled by your fear?

- Do you have any reservations about following through with the steps that you will cover in this book?

- How can you overcome your reservations?

- How will you reward yourself (on a weekly basis) as you challenge yourself to practice the strategies in this book?

After you have answered these questions, the next step is to consider what change will mean for you.

What Are the Benefits and Costs of Change for You?

Any change can have both benefits and costs. Sometimes it is easy to make a change; other times it is harder. It's important to examine the benefits and costs of change so you are prepared for the impact change will have on your life. A major benefit that most people with panic describe is that they start to gain control of their life and begin to feel back to "normal" again—back to feeling that they can do things without concerns about panicking or feeling anxious, or questioning their ability to cope in a situation.

Exercise: Benefits of Changing

Think about what the benefits of change are for you and record your answers to the questions below in your journal.

- What are your reasons, motivations, or inspirations for following through with the changes that will be outlined in this book?

- Why will it be worth it for you to follow through with the strategies you will learn, even if they cause you to feel more anxiety initially?

- What aspects of your life will improve if you are able to overcome your panic attacks and anxiety?

One of the costs of treatment is that you may feel more anxiety and discomfort initially, before you have mastered the strategies in this book. The coping strategies you have developed for panic have worked in the short term. For example, behaviors such as escaping from situations when you feel anxious, distracting yourself from anxiety-provoking feelings, ensuring that you are accompanied by a "safe" person, and avoiding anxiety-provoking situations altogether are easy ways to decrease your fear. Although these coping strategies work in the short term, they are onerous to maintain. We call these behaviors "quick-fix" strategies for coping with anxiety. Over time, these strategies are costly in terms of your comfort, freedom, control, independence, and ultimately, your confidence. In the long term, these quick-fix strategies don't work, and that is why you're reading this book.

One of the ironies of overcoming problems with panic is the requirement that one must initially experience fear in order to conquer fear down the road. As you begin to eliminate your quick-fix strategies, you will not yet have mastered the alternative, helpful strategies that we will cover in this book. So you need to be prepared to experience some anxiety and discomfort in the short term for the long-term goal of conquering your panic. It's a case of "short-term pain for long-term gain," at least with respect to overcoming panic. Paying attention to your anxiety and panic symptoms (a necessary step toward overcoming panic attacks) may lead to increased levels of anxiety, fear, and panic initially. Be patient. Your symptoms will eventually improve.

Exercise: Costs of Changing

Think about what the costs of change are for you and record your answers to the questions below in your journal.

- What are the potential costs of change for you?

- What challenges will you have to overcome in order to follow through with the strategies that are outlined in this book?

- What obstacles may you encounter as you work on overcoming your panic?

In addition to the increased anxiety that you may experience when you begin to work on your panic, another potential cost of treatment is the disruption it may have in terms of your family functioning. Often, family members do things to protect their loved ones from feeling anxious. This process, sometimes called *accommodation*, may involve taking over more and more family roles and responsibilities, so the individual who suffers from panic attacks can avoid feeling panicky. Common ways in which family members may accommodate to an individual's symptoms include:

- No longer going out to eat in restaurants

- Choosing seats that are on the aisle or near an exit

- Avoiding crowded venues or activities

- Taking over responsibilities such as grocery shopping or driving children to activities

- Always carrying a cell phone or pager so they are accessible at all times

- Not taking a vacation that is far from home or out of the "safe zone"

- Accompanying a person who is frightened to go somewhere alone

- Avoiding work trips where they may need to leave town for a few days

Family roles also shift as individuals begin to overcome their anxiety. Consider the following example. Kathleen had lived with her panic disorder for over twenty years. Her anxiety robbed her of her independence, and she felt unable to manage the small tasks of everyday life such as grocery shopping, driving, or even walking by herself. She needed her husband to drive her for the shopping, or accompany her if she wanted to go for a walk. She felt very comfortable when she was with her husband but anxious and panicky when she was alone. For Kathleen, recovery from panic involved taking small steps toward becoming more independent in her life. She practiced walking in her neighborhood alone, being at home alone, and going to the corner store alone. As she became more comfortable in these situations, her independence grew and she challenged herself with bigger tasks. As Kathleen recovered from panic, her entire life changed directions. Although her husband was happy for the steps that she had made, he felt his role in the family had changed and that Kathleen no longer needed him in the way she used to. For Kathleen, recovery from panic meant that her relationship with her husband had to be rebalanced.

Exercise: Family Accommodation

Think about the role your family members may play in allowing you to escape or avoid the situations and symptoms you fear. The longer you have suffered from panic attacks, the more you may notice that the people who are important to you have taken over certain roles to accommodate your anxiety. Although their efforts are helpful in the short term, in the long term these behaviors help to maintain your anxiety and fear. In your journal, answer the following questions:

- What roles or family functions have you given up or reduced because of your panic and anxiety?

- What efforts does your family make to help you keep your anxiety at a manageable level?

- What are the different ways that your family members accommodate your symptoms (helping you to avoid certain situations)?

- As you begin to overcome your anxiety, how might your family relationships be affected?

Your Short-Term and Long-Term Goals

It's helpful to think of recovery from panic in terms of steps. The small steps are your short-term goals. Short-term goals may include resuming activities that have been put on hold, reducing avoidance, and learning strategies to manage panic attacks. The big steps are your long-term goals. These are the steps that will not be reached overnight, but that may be reached as a result of taking many small steps, thereby achieving more and more of your short-term goals. Long-term goals may include returning to work after a long absence, increasing your confidence, reducing your anticipatory anxiety, feeling more comfortable with physical sensations, and for some people, feeling back to your "normal" self.

When Jack came for treatment, he described feeling as though anxiety and panic were controlling his life. He no longer felt like the person he used to be—an independent, confident, and capable professional who supervised nine people. Because of his fear of panic attacks, Jack no longer felt comfortable being alone. He only felt safe if he was with his wife or the few friends who knew what he was going through. He began missing work because he felt so anxious and out of control. Jack feared that he might be "losing it" or going crazy. He felt weak as a person because every little task had become a big challenge for him. Merely going to the store or out for a drive was a major ordeal because of his anxiety.

When we discussed Jack's goals for treatment he stated that he just wanted to be able to wake up in the morning and not worry about how he would feel that day, whether he would be able to manage, or how he would cope. These were reasonable long-term goals. They wouldn't happen overnight, but they would be realized as Jack began to practice the strategies that would help him to overcome his panic. After some discussion about his goals, Jack's short-term goals were established. He planned to learn about panic disorder and how it was affecting him. He planned to follow the treatment suggestions and to practice the strategies while keeping an open mind. He prepared himself to feel some discomfort as he worked toward these goals.

It's important when you set your goals that you make them *specific* rather than *vague*. If goals are too vague, it will

be unclear what steps you will need to take to achieve them. When goals are specific, it is much easier to decide what steps are needed to accomplish the goals, and much easier to know whether the goals have been achieved. Consider the examples below.

Vague Goals

- To feel better in the morning
- To feel less anxious when going out
- To get back my normal life
- To regain control of my emotions

Specific Goals

- To be able to drive to the mall
- To go grocery shopping alone
- To play golf with my friends
- To no longer experience panic attacks on airplanes

Exercise: Setting Goals

Take some time now to consider your goals (remember to be specific) and to answer the following questions in your journal:

- What are your long-term goals?
- What are your short-term goals?
- What are the potential obstacles that may interfere with you achieving your goals?
- What steps can you take to overcome the obstacles you have identified?

Keeping Your Expectations Realistic

The majority of people with panic disorder who seek treatment do so in hopes of eliminating anxiety and panic from their lives. Of course, treatment cannot eliminate all anxiety. In fact, we wouldn't want to do that because anxiety and fear have important functions in your life. These responses help to prepare you to manage future threat and to protect you when you're confronted with an immediate danger. Eliminating fear completely is not a realistic (or even desirable) goal. If you keep your expectations realistic, you will be much more likely to achieve your goals.

It is realistic to expect that this treatment will teach you strategies to take back control of your life. Although you will not eliminate anxiety and fear completely, you will likely be much less afraid of what is happening to your body during a panic attack and much more confident that you will be able to cope in situations that now make you anxious. You will also learn new ways of responding to your anxiety. Finally, by using the strategies described in this book, you will likely reach a point where your anxiety and fear are reduced to a level where they no longer upset you and no longer interfere with your life.

For some people, just practicing the strategies in this book will be enough to overcome their panic disorder. For others, a more intensive treatment approach may be required. As we reviewed in the introduction, there are a number of options available if the strategies described in this book aren't enough, including seeking out additional reading and obtaining professional help from a therapist or doctor who is experienced in these treatments.

Exercise: Making a Contract

Now that you have considered your commitment to change, reviewed the benefits and costs of overcoming your panic, and set your goals, it's time to make a contract with yourself. In your journal, record your answers to the following questions:

- Are you ready to commit to using the treatment strategies described in this book?

- What time period are you willing to set aside to implement this plan (we recommend that you commit for a minimum period of twelve weeks)?

- When things get tough, what supports will you rely on to keep you motivated and on track? For example, can your spouse, a family member, or a close friend provide the encouragement you need to get through the exercises described in this book?

- How will you reward yourself for each week that you put in toward your recovery?

Track Your Panic Symptoms

N ow that you are committed to making a change, the first step is to track your experiences of panic and anxiety so that you can learn about your pattern of symptoms and the situations that trigger them. Be prepared to feel more anxious as you focus on your fears and anxiety, but remember that this anxiety will be temporary and will gradually improve as you learn the strategies in this book. Remember the reasons for following through with this change that you identified in chapter 2. These reasons will help you to hang in there and to continue using the treatment strategies, even when your anxiety is high.

Breaking Down Your Anxiety and Panic

Panic and anxiety often feel uncontrollable and overwhelming. One helpful strategy for dealing with panic is to break it down into more manageable components that can each be targeted directly. These include a physical component (what you *feel* during panic), a cognitive component (what you *think*), and a behavioral component (what you *do*).

THE PHYSICAL COMPONENT

The physical component of panic is an obvious one. When most people think about their panic attacks, they think about the intense physical sensations they experience. It's not surprising that many people who have panic attacks end up at their local emergency room or at their doctor's office because they are convinced there must be something terribly wrong with them. The physical component includes all of the symptoms that occur in your body when you are feeling panicky, as described earlier.

Exercise: The Physical Component

In your journal, record the different physical sensations and symptoms that you tend to experience when you feel panicky or anxious. Common physical symptoms may include: dizziness, racing or pounding heart, chest pain, shortness of breath, feeling of choking, lightheadedness or feeling faint, tingling or numbness sensations, feeling unreal or detached from your body or what is happening around you, hot flushes or chills, sweating, trembling or shakiness, and blurry vision.

THE COGNITIVE COMPONENT

The second component of panic is the cognitive component, which includes any thoughts that run through your mind when you feel anxious. Thoughts may take the form of predictions about bad things that might happen (like losing control or "freaking out"), beliefs about your ability or inability to cope with a situation, your expectations about how a situation will unfold, or mental images of catastrophic consequences (like visually seeing yourself running out of a crowded room or passing out in a meeting at work). Examples of common beliefs regarding panic include:

- If I panic, I will pass out.

- If I don't get out of here, I will go crazy from anxiety.

- I won't be able to cope if I try it on my own.

- This panic could continue forever.

- I will never feel normal again.

- Anxiety means I am weak.

- People will notice that I'm anxious.

Another feature of the cognitive component of panic is the tendency to pay extra close attention to information that confirms your anxious beliefs and to ignore information that disconfirms your beliefs. People with panic disorder tend to scan their bodies for the sensations they fear, are very attuned to their physical feelings, and are often frightened when they notice the sensations that they're looking for. They may also be prone to remembering information particularly well when it confirms their anxious beliefs. For example, they may find it difficult to forget the details of how Ahmad Harris, a twenty-two-year-old college football player, died suddenly of a massive heart attack in 2002. The story may even be misinterpreted as support for the belief that exercise is dangerous.

Exercise: The Cognitive Component

In your journal, record the most common thoughts, beliefs, and interpretations that tend to contribute to your own feelings of panic and anxiety. Examples may include concerns about going crazy, losing control, or dying; fear of having a heart attack or passing out; fear of vomiting or having diarrhea; fear of not being able to escape from a situation or to get help; and fear of being embarrassed or of other people noticing your anxiety.

THE BEHAVIORAL COMPONENT

The third component of panic is the behavioral component. The behavioral component involves what you do when you feel panicky and what you do to avoid feeling panicky. Common behavioral responses include escaping from the situation (for instance, leaving your filled shopping cart in the aisle and leaving the supermarket because of a panic attack) or avoiding a situation altogether (like only going shopping when you're with someone with whom you feel comfortable or canceling plans to go out because you are "not feeling well"). There is a range of other behavioral responses that people have when they are feeling anxious. Some examples include:

- Distraction (for instance, making conversation while waiting in a line, singing a song in your head to avoid thinking about your anxiety, playing the radio while driving so you don't have to focus on how you are feeling)

- Carrying certain items (like medication, cell phone, a bag, or water) with you to feel safe

- Sitting in the aisle seat at a movie or at the back of a theater so you can escape more easily in the event of a panic attack

- Using alcohol or other substances (like marijuana) to manage your anxiety

As an illustration of how panic attacks can influence behavior, consider the example of Gail. When Gail experienced a panic attack, she had uncomfortable stomach distress and the feeling that she would have diarrhea. Although she had never actually had an "accident" during a panic attack, she had persistent anxiety that she would. Gail began to carry an anti-diarrhea medication just in case she began to feel panicky, which she believed could cause her to have diarrhea. Gail also avoided drinking coffee and eating breakfast on mornings when she had to go out so if she did have a panic attack, she wouldn't have eaten anything that could lead to diarrhea. Gail began avoiding a range of activities including eating out in restaurants and socializing with friends because she never knew how she would feel. She also avoided activities where a bathroom was not present or easily accessible, such as her daughter's soccer games, playing golf with her husband, and driving long distances in the country. Gail's fear of having a panic attack translated into significant avoidance in many areas of her life. Her behaviors included both obvious avoidance (no longer socializing) and more subtle forms of avoidance (carrying medication and not eating certain foods). Gail's avoidance ultimately affected her social relationships, her job, her relationships with her husband and children, her mood, and her opinion of herself.

Exercise: The Behavioral Component

In your journal, record the most common behaviors that you use to avoid feeling panicky or to reduce your feelings of panic when they occur. This should include a list of situations that you tend to avoid completely, as well as a list of subtle ways in which you avoid (like making sure you always have someone with you, leaving an event early, sitting in a particular location, distracting yourself, using alcohol to cope, and carrying safety items such as medication, a cell phone, or water).

Interactions Among the Three Components

The physical, cognitive, and behavioral components of panic interact with one another, and any one of these components can trigger changes in the others. For example, Marc was sitting in a meeting at work when he noticed his heart pounding (physical component). This triggered a number of thoughts: "What if I panic right now? I would have to leave the meeting, and people would think there was something wrong with me. If I panic and don't get out in time, I could have a heart attack" (cognitive component). He started to focus more on his physical sensations and less on the meeting going on around him (cognitive component). He started to sweat and feel "unreal" (physical component). He thought to himself: "This is getting worse. I have to get out of here before something terrible happens" (cognitive component). He then left the meeting (behavioral component). As soon as Marc left the room, he noticed that his physical symptoms of anxiety were greatly reduced (physical component).

From this example, you can see that thoughts can make physical sensations worse, and in turn, physical sensations can fuel increased anxious thoughts. Behavioral responses can also serve to increase anxious thoughts and feelings. The treatment strategies that we outline in this book are specifically designed to target these three components to place you back in control.

Exercise: Tracking the Three Components of Panic

To become proficient at identifying your panic triggers and to develop an understanding of the components of your own anxiety and panic, use a new page in your journal to record the following pieces of information, each time you feel anxious over the next week.

- **Situation.** Take note of the situation you were in when you became anxious, fearful, or panicky. What were you doing? Where were you? Who were you with? Are you aware of any triggers (something that happened to you, a sensation you felt) for your anxiety?

- **Level of fear or anxiety.** Record the intensity of your fear or anxiety using a scale from 0 to 100 where "0" indicates that you were not experiencing any anxiety or fear at all and "100" indicates that you were experiencing the worst anxiety or panic that you can imagine feeling.

- **Physical sensations.** What physical sensations did you experience in your body?

- **Anxious thoughts.** What thoughts were going through your mind? What were you afraid might happen? What were your anxious predictions regarding the situation? What were your expectations regarding your coping abilities?

- **Anxious behaviors.** What did you do in the situation? How did you react? Did you use safety behaviors? Did you escape from the situation? Did you avoid it altogether?

After you have recorded your anxiety and panic for a week, take a look back through your journal and record your answers to the following questions:

- What did you learn about the triggers or situations that are associated with feeling anxious or panicky? Did you notice any patterns? Did any of your panic episodes seem to be triggered by a physical symptom?

- Was there a pattern to the symptoms or fearful thoughts that you experienced when you felt anxious or panicky?

- What was the worst thing that happened when you felt anxious or panicky? Did your fearful predictions come true?

- When your anxiety was at its worst, how long (for example, thirty seconds, a few minutes, ten minutes, twenty minutes, etc.) did it typically last before it started to decrease?

Tracking Your Moods

You may have noticed that your panic attacks affect your moods. For example, you may feel increased sadness and hopelessness about whether things will change, and you may think of yourself using negative terms such as "weak," "useless," or "incapable." Because people with panic disorder avoid situations that they associate with panic, they are often deprived of the experiences that are important in their lives and that give them pleasure. It's not uncommon for people with panic disorder to develop symptoms of depression. In fact, for some individuals, the depression may be present even before the onset of panic attacks.

As you follow through with the treatment strategies outlined in this book, you will likely notice your moods improving. You will begin to reengage in the activities you have been avoiding, and you will begin to feel more effective and better about yourself.

Exercise: Tracking your Moods

Over the next week, use your journal to monitor your levels of anxiety and depression. At the end of each day, record the following:

- Your average level of anxiety for the day, using the 0 to 100 scale described earlier

- Your average level of depression for the day, using a 0 to 100 scale where "0" indicates that you were not at all depressed and "100" indicates that you were feeling as depressed as you can imagine feeling

- Any negative thoughts that you had about yourself, others, or your future

- What is the connection between your anxiety and your depression?

- What were your highest levels of anxiety and depression over the week?

- What were your lowest levels of anxiety and depression over the week?

- How did your thoughts vary depending on fluctuations in the intensity of your anxiety and depression?

After you have monitored your depression and anxiety for a week, examine your responses and answer the following questions in your journal:

- What is the connection between your anxiety and your depression?

- What were your highest levels of anxiety and depression over the week?

- What were your lowest levels of anxiety and depression over the week?

How did your thoughts vary depending on fluctuations in the intensity of your anxiety and depression?

Replace Anxious Thinking with Realistic Thinking

What if you were absolutely sure that your panic symptoms were *not* dangerous? If you knew with 100 percent confidence that you would not die, have a heart attack, go crazy, lose control, vomit, have diarrhea, or make a fool of yourself during an attack, would you still be afraid of having panic attacks? If you were somehow guaranteed that your panic attacks would not go on indefinitely but would always end before long, would you continue to be fearful of panicking? If you completely sure that the worst thing that could happen during a panic attack was that you would feel temporarily uncomfortable, would you still fear panic? As we reviewed earlier, it's not the panic attacks themselves that are the biggest problem for people who suffer from panic disorder. Rather, it is the beliefs that people hold about their panic attacks and their fear of panic that cause so much trouble. It is these scary, negative predictions that lead people to worry about having more attacks, scan their bodies for panic-related symptoms, react to normal physical sensations (such as racing heart and dizziness) with extreme fear, and avoid situations that have become associated with panic.

If you can learn to be less concerned about having panic attacks, you will most certainly begin to experience panic less frequently. In fact, as soon as you are truly willing to experience the attacks, in all likelihood they will go away. The goal of this chapter is to help you to begin viewing your panic attacks as nothing more than brief periods of discomfort (like a headache, a sore knee, or a bad rash), rather than a source of danger or threat.

Research into Anxious Thinking

After two decades of research on the role of anxious thinking in triggering and maintaining panic disorder, it is now well established that panic attacks are influenced by a person's beliefs, interpretations, and other cognitive processes. Consider the following research findings:

- Numerous studies have found that people with panic disorder experience high levels of fear in response to normal symptoms of physical arousal, including increased heart rate, dizziness, and breathlessness (Chambless and Gracely 1989; Taylor, Koch, and McNally 1992).

- Some researchers have found that people with panic disorder are more likely than others to be aware of their heart beats (van der Does, Antony, Barsky, and Ehlers 2000).

- People with panic disorder are more likely than nonanxious individuals to shift their attention toward uncomfortable physical sensations when they occur (Ehlers and Breuer 1995), and they even focus more intensely on words that are related to panic symptoms, such as "heart" and "palpitation" (Ehlers, Margraf, Davies, and Roth 1988).

- People with panic disorder are more likely than their nonanxious counterparts to remember threat-related words (McNally, Hornig, Otto, and Pollack 1997), and they are more likely to remember having seen photographs of faces that they had previously rated as "safe" (faces of people who seem like they could be counted on if needed) (Lundh, Thulin, Czyzykow, and Öst 1998).

- Compared to people without an anxiety problem, people with panic disorder are more likely to interpret physical symptoms as a sign of some immediate catastrophe (like a heart attack or going crazy), especially when they don't know what is causing the symptoms (Clark et al. 1997).

- People with panic disorder tend to overestimate the actual likelihood of having panic attacks in the situations they fear (Schmidt, Jacquin, and Telch 1994). Furthermore, some researchers have found that the expectation that one will panic is associated with a greater likelihood of actually panicking (Kenardy and Taylor 1999).

In summary, there is very strong evidence that panic disorder is associated with a stronger-than-usual tendency to pay attention to physical symptoms, to remember information that is consistent with one's anxious beliefs, and to misinterpret physical symptoms as being dangerous. Not surprisingly, the more frightened you are of particular physical feelings, the more you will tend to notice these symptoms, in part because you're looking for them. And if you're looking for symptoms, you'll probably find them. That may be why noticing another person yawning can trigger your own feeling of having to yawn.

Exercise: The Effects of Paying Attention to Your Body

For the next sixty seconds, turn your attention to your body and scan the surface of your skin until you find an itch. Stop reading now until you have completed this task.

Now, on a new page in your journal, record responses to the following questions. How long did it take to locate an itch on your skin? Do you think you would have noticed the itch if you weren't specifically looking for it? What does this experience tell you about the relationship between whether you are looking for a symptom and whether you then experience the symptom? Can you think of times in your life when you noticed an uncomfortable physical feeling, reacted to it with fear, and ended up in a state of panic? This exercise was designed to demonstrate that just looking for a symptom may be enough to trigger an awareness of the sensation.

Anxious Thinking

In order to reduce the frequency of your panic attacks, it's important to change the way you think about panic and about the symptoms you fear. But first, you must become more aware of the types of thoughts that trigger your own panic attacks. In all likelihood, you have been experiencing anxiety and panic for some time. If so, many of the thoughts underlying your panic attacks may occur automatically—so quickly that you are not even aware of them. If this is true, identifying your anxious thoughts will take some practice.

In this section, we discuss two types of anxious thinking that are believed to contribute significantly to the anxiety and fear experienced by people with panic disorder (Craske and Barlow 2001). We refer to these types of thinking as *overestimating probabilities* and *overestimating the severity of consequences*.

OVERESTIMATING PROBABILITIES

Overestimating probabilities involves predicting that a particular event is more likely to occur than it really is. A typical example of a probability overestimation in panic disorder is the belief that certain panic symptoms (for instance, a pounding or racing heart, tightness in the chest, dizziness, difficulty breathing) are an indication of heart disease or an impending heart attack. Although it's true that heart attacks are sometimes associated with these symptoms, there are many other factors that are more typically responsible for triggering these sensations, including focusing one's attention on the body, breathing too quickly or too deeply, physical exercise, sexual arousal, caffeine, nicotine, alcohol withdrawal, hormonal changes, anxiety, fear, excitement, and other intense emotions. And yet, it is not unusual for someone who suffers from panic disorder to automatically assume that cardiac symptoms are a sign of heart disease, even when previous panic attacks have never ended in a heart attack, and even when the individual may have few of the risk factors for heart disease (for example, advanced age, high blood pressure, elevated cholesterol, obesity, smoking, or a family history of heart disease).

Other common examples of beliefs that involve overestimating probabilities include:

- If I get dizzy, I will faint.

- I will have diarrhea in a public place.

- My next panic attack may never end.
- If I don't leave the situation when I have a panic attack, I will surely lose control.
- If my panic attacks continue, I could go crazy.
- The only reason why I didn't throw up during my last panic attack is because I sat down and rested.
- If I'm not careful, I could die from a panic attack.

Some of these statements are completely untrue (for example, nobody ever dies or goes crazy as a result of panic attacks), whereas others are simply exaggerations of the actual probabilities. For example, although it is extremely rare for dizziness to lead to fainting, it is possible. Fainting during fear is actually quite common among people with blood and needle phobias (see Antony and Swinson 2000), though it's very unusual among people with panic disorder.

Exercise: Recording Overestimations of Probability

To become more aware of your own probability overestimations, try answering the following questions each time you feel anxious or each time you feel an urge to avoid a situation or escape from a situation. Repeat this exercise whenever you feel anxious for at least the next few weeks, until identifying your probability overestimations becomes second nature. Record your responses in your journal.

- What am I afraid might happen?

- What might happen if I don't leave the situation?

- What would the outcome be of entering the situation and staying there?

- What terrible things am I predicting will occur?

OVERESTIMATING SEVERITY OF CONSEQUENCES

Overestimating the severity of consequences involves assuming that a particular outcome would be much worse than it really would be. This type of thinking is sometimes referred to as *catastrophizing* or *catastrophic thinking,* and it is associated with a tendency to exaggerate the importance of whether a specific prediction comes true. Examples of overestimating the severity of consequences include the following statements:

- It would be a disaster if I were to panic in a movie theater.

- If I have a panic attack, I won't be able to cope.

- I must do everything I can to avoid experiencing a panic attack or else something horrible will happen.

- The thought of getting stuck in an elevator is one of the worst things I can imagine.

- When I have a panic attack, it's essential that I have someone with me in case I become incapacitated.

- I would not be able to manage if I were to have a panic attack at work.

- It would be terrible to faint, throw up, or have diarrhea.

Although most of these consequences would be uncomfortable, they would probably be much more manageable than you think, and they would pass before you know it. Can you think of examples from your own life when you exaggerated the possible consequences of panicking or of being stuck in a situation you fear? The exercise below is designed to help you identify examples of catastrophic thinking.

Exercise: Recording Overestimations of Consequences

To become more aware of your tendencies to overestimate how bad particular outcomes might be, try answering the following question each time you feel anxious or each time you feel as though you must avoid a situation or escape from a situation: Am I predicting that a particular event will be more catastrophic or unmanageable than it likely will be? In five years from now, will I still be thinking about this particular event? Continue this exercise for at least a few weeks, until identifying your catastrophic thoughts becomes second nature. Record your responses in your journal.

Changing Your Anxious Thinking

In the 1960s, a number of influential psychologists and psychiatrists (including Aaron T. Beck, Albert Ellis, and others) began to develop strategies for changing negative thinking with the goal of alleviating anxiety, depression, and related problems. Since then, a number of other individuals (including psychologists David M. Clark, David H. Barlow, Michele Craske, Ron Rapee, and others) have refined these techniques and have demonstrated through extensive research that cognitive strategies are effective for combating problems with panic and associated fears (for a review, see Antony and Swinson 2000). In this section, we present some of the most powerful cognitive methods for combating anxious thinking, including examining the evidence for and against your anxious predictions, challenging catastrophic thoughts, and conducting behavioral experiments.

EXAMINING THE EVIDENCE

Examining the evidence involves considering all of the available information in order to arrive at a realistic conclusion regarding whether your original anxious thought is true. Although it may be easy to come up with evidence supporting your negative predictions, thinking of reasons why your anxious thought may not be true is often more difficult. This is because of the natural tendency for people to give greater weight to information that supports their beliefs than to information that contradicts their beliefs. Below are examples of questions that you can ask yourself in order to come up with evidence supporting your anxious prediction, as well as evidence that suggests your anxious thought may not be true:

- Do I know for sure that my prediction will come true?

- Have I made similar predictions in the past? If so, how often do my panic-related thoughts come true?

- Are there any other ways of thinking about this situation (for example, is a feeling of unreality necessarily a sign that I am going crazy? Or, is dizziness always an indication that I am about to faint)?

- What are some other reasons for this feeling I'm experiencing?

- Do I have any proof that my panic attacks are dangerous?

- How long do my panic attacks usually last?

- What might a supportive friend or relative tell me if they knew I was having these anxious thoughts?

As you try to answer questions such as these, make sure that you consider evidence on both sides of the issue. This is crucial for coming to as balanced a conclusion as possible. Consider the following example:

- **Anxious belief:** I will pass out if I get too dizzy during a panic attack.

- **Evidence in support of belief:** When people pass out, they usually feel very dizzy or lightheaded beforehand. The feeling I get during my panic attacks is very similar to what I imagine I would feel if I were to pass out. The only reason I haven't passed out before is because I usually lie down during my attacks.

- **Evidence against belief:** I have had more than 100 panic attacks over the past few years, and I have never passed out, even during those times when I was unable to lie down. Every book that I read about panic disorder mentions that although many people with panic disorder fear passing out during their attacks, it is very unusual for panic attacks to actually cause fainting. Fainting is usually caused by a sudden drop in blood pressure and heart rate, but panic attacks are typically associated with increased heart rate and blood pressure—the very opposite reaction of what normally occurs during fainting. If I am one of those rare individuals who actually is at risk for passing out during a panic attack, it probably would have happened by now.

- **Rational conclusion**: Although there is a small chance that I could pass out during a panic attack, the likelihood of it happening is very small, no matter how dizzy I feel.

Here is another example:

- **Anxious belief**: If I keep having panic attacks, I will probably go crazy.

- **Evidence in support of belief**: When I feel panicky, things don't seem quite right. I feel unreal, as though I'm in a dreamlike state, and sometimes I even feel as though I am looking at myself from outside my body. Panic disorder is considered a "mental disorder," so if I am having panic attacks, it's just a matter of time before I completely lose touch with reality. I feel completely out of control during my attacks, and perhaps this is the first step toward going crazy.

- **Evidence against belief**: Although feeling out of control and afraid of going crazy are common features of panic attacks, people with panic disorder do not lose touch with reality. Schizophrenia (a disorder in which individuals lose touch with reality, involving both hallucinations and delusional thoughts) is not related to panic disorder. These two problems do not run in the same family (suggesting a different genetic basis for each), and they respond to different treatments. Furthermore, although panic disorder is technically considered a mental disorder according to the American Psychiatric Association, so is the inability to quit smoking (nicotine dependence), being afraid of spiders (specific phobia), and not being able to sleep (insomnia), and I certainly don't consider people with these problems to be mentally ill. Feelings of unreality and depersonalization are common symptoms during panic attacks, and all my reading tells me that these symptoms are not signs of a more serious problem. Finally, although I feel like I am losing control during my attacks, I don't really lose control. I don't scream out in public, I don't make a fool of myself, and I don't run away. In fact, people usually assure me that they don't even notice when I'm having a panic attack unless I tell them what I am going through.

- **Rational conclusion**: Nobody has ever gone crazy from a panic attack, and I am unlikely to go crazy, no matter how uncomfortable I may feel when the attack is occurring.

Exercise: Examining the Evidence

Next time you experience a panic attack or elevated anxiety, examine the evidence to challenge negative predications that enter your mind. In your journal, record your anxious prediction, the evidence that supports your belief, the evidence against your belief, and your rational conclusion based on the evidence. Repeat this exercise whenever you feel anxious or panicky over the next few weeks. With practice, this strategy should become second nature, so eventually you can review the evidence in your head without relying on your journal.

OVERCOMING CATASTROPHIC THINKING

Overcoming catastrophic thinking involves asking yourself questions to examine the realistic impact of a feared outcome in the event that it actually were to occur. A reminder—these strategies are meant to be used to combat a tendency to overestimate the *impact* of some negative consequence (for instance, "It would be unbearable to have a panic attack at work"), not the tendency to overestimate the likelihood of something bad happening ("I will have a heart attack"). To combat probability overestimations, it is more useful to examine the evidence, as described earlier. To combat catastrophic thinking, it's important to start asking yourself questions such as these:

- What's the worst thing that will happen in this situation?

- How can I cope with this situation if it were to occur? How have I coped with it in the past?

- Would the consequences really be as bad as I am predicting?

- So what if I have a panic attack?

- If my feared prediction comes true, will it still matter the next day? How about a week later, or even a year later?

Let's review some of the catastrophic thoughts listed earlier in the chapter, this time adding the step of challenging these beliefs with a more rational response.

- **Catastrophic thought:** It would be a disaster if I were to panic in a movie theater.

- **Rational response:** What's the worst that would happen? If I were to panic, I could just sit in my seat and wait for the attack to end. It would probably last anywhere from a few minutes to a half hour. The worst that would happen is I would feel uncomfortable. In all likelihood, nobody would notice. If my squirming and shaking is disturbing to my neighbor, I could always leave the theater for a short time. No matter how bad the attack feels, it would eventually end.

- **Catastrophic thought:** The thought of getting stuck in an elevator and panicking is one of the worst things I can imagine.

- **Rational response:** Do I know anyone who has ever been stuck in an elevator? If so, is the person still stuck? Of course not! Everyone who gets stuck in elevators eventually gets unstuck. Nobody dies from being stuck in an elevator. Even if I were to get trapped, it would only be for a short time. I might feel very uncomfortable, but my panic would eventually end. Other than that, the worst outcome is that I would be late for wherever I was going. People would understand if I was late. If I was stuck, the consequence would be that I would have an interesting story to tell later.

- **Catastrophic thought:** It would be terrible to faint, throw up, or have diarrhea.

- **Rational response:** Although it would be uncomfortable to faint, throw up, or have diarrhea, it would be manageable if one of these consequences were to occur. I have seen people faint on a couple of occasions, and the people in the room were very supportive. Although I sometimes have diarrhea during my panic attacks, I always make it to a bathroom in time. In fact, during the times where there was no bathroom around, I was able to resist the urge to go until it finally passed. Most people have times when they have thrown up for one reason or another. If that happened to me, people would be understanding. In fact, if someone wasn't understanding, I wouldn't think much of that person anyway. Eventually, the memory of my throwing up would fade from people's minds.

Exercise: Challenging Catastrophic Thinking

When you notice yourself overestimating the consequences of a particular feared outcome coming true, use the strategies described in this section to combat your catastrophic thinking. In your journal, record your catastrophic thought followed by a few points to remind yourself of how you could manage the situation if it were to occur. As with the other strategies described in this chapter, this process should be ongoing. Repeat this exercise whenever you feel anxious or panicky over the next few weeks. This strategy will eventually seem more natural. At that point, it will be less important to rely on your journal.

BEHAVIORAL EXPERIMENTS

Behavioral experiments involve playing the role of the scientist in order to discover whether your anxious beliefs are true. The first step involves identifying your anxious thought, as well as an alternative, nonanxious thought. The next step is to conduct an experiment to help you to decide which belief is true.

For example, let's assume you fear that panic attacks can lead to heart attacks, and that the only reason you haven't experienced a heart attack during your panic attacks so far is because you have engaged in various behaviors (like distraction, sitting down, breathing exercises, calling a loved one, etc.) to keep your panic symptoms in check. In this example, an alternative belief might be that panic attacks don't lead to heart attacks, and that these behaviors really have no effect on your risk of having a heart attack. Can you think of an experiment that you might conduct to test out which of these beliefs is true? One possibility is to refrain from using your safety behaviors and seeing what happens. Instead of sitting down during your next panic attack, try running up and down the stairs a few times. Instead of trying to slow down your breathing, try breathing at a normal rate, or even increasing your rate of breathing. Instead of distracting yourself from your symptoms, try focusing on your symptoms. In all likelihood, conducting experiments such as these will lead to increased anxiety in the short term. However, if you survive (and of course you will survive), you will learn that your original thought isn't true, which should lead to a decrease in fear the next time you experience panic symptoms.

Here are some ideas for other experiments that can be used to challenge your anxious beliefs.

- **Anxious belief:** My legs will turn to "jelly," and I will collapse.

- **Experiment:** See if you can make yourself collapse. For example, try standing on one leg.

- **Anxious belief:** If my hands shake, people will think there is something wrong with me.

- **Experiment:** Let your hands purposely shake when you are around others. See if anyone even notices.

- **Anxious belief:** If I keep driving during a panic attack, I will swerve into another car.

- **Experiment:** Continue driving despite feeling panicky.

- **Anxious belief:** Activities that make my heart race (like sex or exercise) are dangerous.

- **Experiment:** Turn up the romance with your partner, or try working out on the treadmill.

These activities will likely trigger some anxiety if they are situations that normally make you anxious. However, trying them despite your anxiety will help you to learn whether they are in fact dangerous.

When you are designing behavioral experiments, be sure to only use practices that most people would consider safe. For example, don't drive 100 miles per hour just to see what happens. Similarly, if you've not had a physical exam to rule out medical problems that could be causing your symptoms, get everything checked out first by your family doctor. Once you have a thorough physical and you receive a clean bill of health, it's probably safe to assume that your symptoms are not medically based.

Troubleshooting

The strategies described in this chapter are often difficult to use at first. In this section, we discuss a few of the most common obstacles that people often report, as well as some possible solutions.

Problem: I cannot identify my anxious thoughts.

Solution: Because anxious thoughts are often automatic, they may be difficult to identify at first. With practice, this usually gets easier. Sometimes anxious thoughts are more evident during times of anxiety, so forcing yourself to enter a feared situation may help to make you more aware of your thoughts. If you cannot identify any anxious thoughts at all, you may respond better to the other strategies discussed in the next few chapters of this book.

Problem: I have difficulty believing the "rational" thoughts, even after examining the evidence.

Solution: Make sure you're not examining the evidence in a biased way. For example, make sure that you are not giving more weight to the evidence that supports your anxious beliefs than you are to the evidence that disproves your anxious thoughts. With practice, you will find that your level of belief in the rational thought gradually increases and your level of belief in the anxious thought gradually decreases.

Problem: I have a medical condition (for instance, mitral valve prolapse, seizure disorder, asthma, diabetes, vertigo, irritable bowel syndrome) that contributes to my symptoms.

Solution: Find out from your doctor what the realistic risks and restrictions are from your illness. Also, try to learn ways to distinguish symptoms of your physical illness from symptoms of your panic. Without knowing all the facts, it will be hard to examine the evidence for your thoughts in a balanced and accurate way. With a bit of research, you may discover that you are overestimating the risks from your illness. Remember—most people with mitral valve prolapse, seizure disorder, asthma, diabetes, vertigo, or irritable bowel syndrome learn to manage their symptoms without having panic attacks.

Problem: When I am having a panic attack, I can't think clearly enough to challenge my beliefs.

Solution: If you find it hard to think straight during your panic attacks, you may find it easier to practice challenging your anxious thoughts either before your attack (before entering a feared situation) or after your symptoms have improved. You may want to make up a cue card listing some rational statements that you have come up with by examining your past panic attacks (for example, the worst thing that will happen is I will feel anxious; this panic attack will peak and pass). If you are too anxious to think rationally during a panic attack, you can pull out your cue card and prompt yourself by reading over the rational statements.

Confront Places Where Your Panic Attacks Occur

In chapter 4 we reviewed a number of strategies for becoming more aware of your anxious thoughts and for shifting to a more realistic style of thinking about your panic-related symptoms. Another effective method for overcoming anxious thinking is to confront feared situations directly—to learn beyond a doubt that your predictions of danger simply don't come true. This chapter, as well as chapters 6 and 7, discuss how exposure to the situations and symptoms you fear will lead to significant reductions in anxiety and panic. This chapter provides a general overview of exposure-based treatments, with an emphasis on exposure to feared situations and places (often referred to as *in vivo* or *situational* exposure). In chapter 6 you'll learn more about exposure to feared physical sensations and chapter 7 will be the place to discover the importance of eliminating safety behaviors during your exposure practices.

Avoiding Situations Keeps Your Fear Alive

All organisms prefer to avoid situations that they perceive as dangerous or threatening. This makes sense, because avoiding potential threat increases one's chances of survival. An added benefit of avoidance is that it reduces the likelihood of experiencing uncomfortable emotions such as fear and anxiety, as well as all the physical sensations that go along with these feelings. In other words, people avoid situations because avoidance makes them feel better.

Although avoiding situations that are truly dangerous (like walking in a bad neighborhood at night, raising tigers in your backyard, or driving in a blizzard) is useful, avoiding situations in which the actual danger is minimal can sometimes cause problems, particularly if being in these situations is necessary for you to function well in your work or in your personal life. There are several disadvantages of avoiding agoraphobic situations:

- Avoidance prevents you from learning that the situations you fear are in fact perfectly safe. For example, by avoiding driving on days when you feel panicky, you never really get to learn that you can actually drive quite safely, even when experiencing panicky feelings.

- The relief you feel when you avoid or escape from a situation helps to reinforce your avoidance behavior in the future. The next time you enter the situation and feel uncomfortable, you will likely think back to the last time you escaped and how good it felt to leave. That relief makes you more likely to escape again next time, perpetuating the cycle of avoidance. It's similar to the way someone who is dependent on alcohol may drink to relieve the discomfort caused from a hangover.

- Although you initially feel better when you avoid a situation, you also likely feel guilty, frustrated, and disappointed in yourself for not being able to follow through or engage in the activities that you were able to do previously. Avoidance results in erosion of your self-esteem and self-confidence.

- Although avoidance leads to relief and reduced fear in the short term, it actually helps to maintain your fear over the long term for the reasons listed earlier. Ultimately, to overcome your fear now and for the foreseeable future, you will need to start gradually confronting the situations that trigger your panic attacks. We know this probably sounds scary, but remember that thousands have used this technique to overcome their fears.

Planning for Exposure Therapy

Before you start conducting exposure practices, it is a good idea to do some careful planning. Specifically, you will need to identify the types of situations you fear, identify the factors that influence your fear in these situations, create an exposure hierarchy, and develop an exposure schedule.

IDENTIFYING FEARED SITUATIONS

Most people with panic disorder find it difficult to enter situations unless they are certain they will be able to escape or that they'll be able to get help if necessary. The first step in preparing for exposure therapy involves identifying the situations that you fear and avoid. Chapter 1 includes a list of situations that people with panic disorder often avoid (see the section called "What is Agoraphobia?").

Exercise: Identify Your Feared Situations

To start, review the list of typical agoraphobic situations in chapter 1. Are there any of these situations that you tend to avoid, either when alone or even when accompanied by someone else? In your journal, make a list of the situations that you fear and avoid. If there are any situations that aren't on the list in chapter 1, make sure to include them in your list as well. Beside each entry, record your typical level of fear when confronting the situation, using a scale ranging from 0 (no fear; never avoid) to 100 (as frightened as I can imagine being; would avoid the situation at almost any cost).

IDENTIFYING FACTORS THAT INFLUENCE YOUR FEAR

The next step is to identify the variables that make you feel better or worse in the situations you fear. A few examples of such variables include:

- Whether you are alone or with someone else; who you are with (a safe person versus someone you don't know well)

- Whether escape is easy (for example, being at a party may be easier if you brought your own car and can therefore leave easily)

- How close you are to a bathroom (especially if you are fearful of vomiting or having diarrhea)

- Whether you engage in certain safety behaviors (like carrying medication, a drink, a mobile phone, etc.)

- How close you are to the exit (of a bus, theater, or restaurant)
- Whether you are driving in the left lane or right lane, and whether you are driving on a highway or on city streets
- The time of day

Exercise: Identify Factors that Influence Your Fear

Review the list of feared situations that you generated in the previous exercise. For each situation, make a list in your journal of the variables that affect your fear. For example, if you fear going to shopping malls, your list of influencing variables may include such things as whether the mall is crowded, whether you're alone when you go there, how close you are to the exit, the lighting in the mall, how far from the mall entrance you are parked, how far from home you are, whether you are having a "bad day," whether you have to buy anything, or whether you have your medications with you.

DEVELOPING AN EXPOSURE HIERARCHY

Now that you have generated a list of feared situations and a list of factors that influence how frightened you are in these situations, the next step is to put these lists together and develop an exposure hierarchy. An exposure hierarchy is a list of feared situations (usually ten to fifteen items), rank ordered in terms of difficulty. The most frightening situations go at the top of the hierarchy and the less frightening situations go at the bottom. Below is a sample hierarchy.

Sample Hierarchy	
Situation	**Fear Rating**
Flying to Philadelphia on a full plane, alone	100
Flying to Philadelphia on a full plane with my spouse	95
Driving alone on the highway from work to home at rush hour	95
Driving alone to the Galleria Mall on main streets, in heavy traffic	80
Seeing a movie in a crowded theater with my children	75
Eating in a large, crowded restaurant with my spouse	75
Driving with my spouse on the highway from work to home at rush hour	70
Shopping at the Galleria Mall alone on a Saturday	65
Driving over the Highway 41 Bridge on a Sunday afternoon	60
Walking around the neighborhood alone during the day	50
Getting my haircut, alone, at a slow time	50
Standing in a long line at the bank	45
Driving with my spouse to the Galleria Mall on main streets in light traffic	40
Shopping for groceries at the local supermarket with my spouse	35

Exercise: Develop an Exposure Hierarchy

In your journal, develop your own exposure hierarchy. Include ten to fifteen items with wide ranging levels of difficulty. Be specific. Make sure to indicate the feared situation as well as the most important variables that influence your fear. For example, don't just say "Driving to the store." A more descriptive and useful item would be "Driving to the corner supermarket alone at rush hour." Also, only include items that you could practice if you wanted to. For example, there is no point including "A trip around the world" on your hierarchy if you can't afford to take such a trip anyway. Finally, don't worry about whether you feel ready to try all the items on your hierarchy. At first, chances are that you will only be able to attempt the items on the bottom half of the hierarchy. It is perfectly normal for the top few items to seem impossible at the beginning. Think of your hierarchy as a "wish list" of all the things that you would like to be able to do if you didn't experience panic.

DEVELOPING AN EXPOSURE SCHEDULE

Doing exposure properly takes considerable time and commitment. To get the most benefit from exposure therapy you will need to practice at least a few times per week for a period of a few weeks or months and for a good chunk of time each session. It would be ideal if you set aside ninety minutes to two hours per day to practice. If you can't afford that much time, make sure to schedule practices on at least four days per week.

In many cases, practices can be integrated into your normal routine (for example, driving to work instead of getting a ride from someone else). For other situations on your list, you will need to schedule exposure practices, just as you would any other appointment. One approach that works well for many people is to schedule the entire week's practices at the beginning of each week.

Another approach is to do the exposure more intensively. Instead of practicing for an hour or two each day, some people prefer to completely clear their schedule and make exposure practices their full-time job for a week or two. Whatever approach you take, the most important thing is to remember that the more time you spend doing exposure practices, the greater the reduction in anxiety you will experience and the sooner you will start to see changes in the frequency of your panic attacks.

Guidelines for Conducting Exposure Practices

As you begin to think about confronting the situations that trigger your panic attacks, there may be a number of concerns running through your head. For example, how will you be able to enter the situations on your hierarchy? After all, if you were able to do these things, you wouldn't need to be reading this book. Or, you may be skeptical about whether exposure will work for you. If anything, your past experience tells you that when you enter these situations, you feel worse—not better. The remainder of this chapter will address these and other concerns. In the next section, we review a number of suggestions that will help you to get the most out of your exposure practices. When you follow these suggestions, exposure is one of the most effective ways of overcoming fear.

WHAT TO EXPECT DURING EXPOSURE THERAPY

Although exposure typically leads to a reduction in fear over time, it usually takes a few sessions before you start to notice the benefits. During practices, it is normal for people to feel anxious, and it's not unusual for practices to trigger panic attacks. Between practices you may initially feel more anxious, irritable, and exhausted. Confronting situations that you previously avoided takes some getting used to. Initially, it is important to make a commitment to doing the practices, regardless of how you feel. To reinforce this point, we often use the analogy of physical exercise. When you first begin an exercise regimen, you may notice yourself feeling more tired and sore than usual. It's not until several weeks after beginning to exercise regularly that the benefits start to appear. If you are patient, you will start to notice a reduction in fear over time as well as improvements in your confidence.

The first time you try something new, expect to feel panicky. With each practice, it will most likely get easier. However, don't get discouraged if your fear doesn't *always* decrease from week to week. You may notice that some weeks are better than others. You may have periods during which your panic attacks get slightly worse (especially if you are under stress) even though you are sticking to your practices. Stay with it. Over time, your investment will pay off.

DURATION AND SPACING OF SESSIONS

Two of the most important rules for exposure therapy are first, to stay in the situation until your fear comes down, and second, to schedule your practices close together. Both of these recommendations probably describe the exact opposite of what you want to do when you're feeling panicky, but following these suggestions will be much more helpful than not following them.

If you leave a situation when your fear is at its peak, you learn that when you are in the situation you feel uncomfortable, and when you leave you feel better. Afterward, you may also feel discouraged about not having stayed in the situation. On the other hand, if you stay in the situation despite your fear, you will find that the fear eventually comes down. It may take a few minutes, or it may take a few hours—but it *will* come down. By staying, you will discover that you can actually be in the situation and feel okay. You will also get a much needed boost of confidence. It's not essential to stay until your fear is completely gone. If you notice a significant reduction in fear, and if your discomfort level is manageable, it's okay to end the practice or to move on to the next step in your hierarchy by increasing the intensity of the exposure.

If you find that your fear is completely overwhelming and that you must leave the situation, that's fine. Just try to get back into the situation a few minutes later, once you are feeling more comfortable. Also, if the situation you are practicing is by definition a brief encounter (like driving over a bridge, riding the elevator to your office, or standing in line at a grocery store), it is important to repeat the practice over and over to get the benefits that occur with a more prolonged exposure.

Exposure works best when the practices are spaced close together. For example, a study by psychologist Edna Foa and her colleagues (Foa, Jameson, Turner, and Payne 1980) found that individuals who completed ten sessions of exposure for their agoraphobia had a better outcome if the ten sessions were completed once per day over ten days than if they were completed once per week over ten weeks. Spacing your practices close together allows your gains to build on one another.

If the practices are spaced too far apart, each practice is like starting over and there is less benefit to adding additional practices.

HOW TO SELECT PRACTICES

When you are selecting practices, your hierarchy can be used as a guide. However, you don't have to start by practicing items at the bottom of the hierarchy. If you feel able to try something part way up the list, that's fine. Keep in mind that more difficult items will trigger higher levels of fear, but attempting more difficult items will also help you to overcome the problem more quickly. Ideally, you should be trying practices that are as difficult as you can tolerate without completely overwhelming yourself with feelings of fear and panic.

There are few risks to trying items that are too difficult. The worst that will happen is that you will feel more anxious and may experience a panic attack. If a practice seems too difficult, simply try something that is a bit easier. For example, if driving alone at rush hour in the left lane of the highway leads to overwhelming panic, try driving in the right lane, or with your spouse, or at a less busy time.

When selecting practices from your hierarchy, it is perfectly acceptable to skip some items on the list, to practice items out of order, or even to select practices that are not on the list at all. The hierarchy is meant to be used flexibly, as a rough guide.

PREDICTABILITY AND CONTROL

Most people with panic disorder feel as though they have little control over their panic attacks, and there is usually no way to predict when an attack will occur. Therefore, it is no wonder that the fear of panicking continues to be so strong, despite repeated exposure to the symptoms during the course of typical panic attacks. Unpredictable and uncontrollable exposure to a feared situation often leads to increased levels of fear over time.

However, predictable exposure that you can control has exactly the opposite effect. Therefore, it is useful to plan your exposures in advance, to consider the possible effects of exposure (like increased panic symptoms) so there are no surprises, and to plan practices so you have control over when they start and when they stop. For example, if a family member is helping you practice by driving you around town, the person should understand that you are in charge. He or she should not do anything (for instance, change lanes, or increase the intensity of the practice) without first getting your permission.

WHAT TO DO DURING EXPOSURE PRACTICES

There are a few additional strategies that you can use to make your exposure practices a success. First, try not to rely on safety behaviors, such as distraction, having a glass of wine, or sitting near the exit. This issue is discussed in detail in chapter 7. If you need to use these behaviors early in treatment, that's fine. However, try to reduce their use as your fear improves.

Second, expect to feel anxious. Often, people feel as though their exposure practice was a failure if they experienced anxiety or panic during the practice. In reality, a successful practice is one in which you become anxious and stay in the situation despite your anxiety. You are supposed to be uncomfortable during exposure practices. Don't be surprised when it happens.

Third, try not to fight your fear. Fighting your fear is sort of like fighting to fall asleep. If you lie in bed for hours saying to yourself, "I must fall asleep!" you can end up keeping yourself awake all night. Sometimes, the more you try to fall asleep, the harder it is to actually fall asleep. Similarly, the more you try to make your panic symptoms go away, the more you will keep them around, or even make them worse. Instead, just let your fear happen. If anything, welcome a panic attack if it occurs. Think about each panic attack as an opportunity to practice your new strategies. It may sound paradoxical, but if you can reach a point where you can welcome the panic attacks, they will no longer occur.

Finally, use the cognitive coping strategies that you learned in chapter 4. If you notice anxious thoughts entering your mind during exposure practices, examine the evidence supporting these thoughts, as well as the evidence supporting alternative, nonanxious thoughts. Ask yourself, "So what if I panic?" and engage in behavioral experiments to test out the validity of your anxious thoughts. Exposure practices are the perfect context in which to use the cognitive techniques described in the preceding chapter.

A Sample Exposure Session

Rachel was a thirty-five-year-old teacher who had been suffering from panic disorder and agoraphobia for more than ten years. She experienced panic attacks about once per week, and she avoided many situations, including crowded places, public transportation, and driving. Her fear was much worse when she was alone. In the early part of her treatment, she had been working on spending more time in crowded places such as restaurants, supermarkets, and malls, with some success. She was also able to reduce her fear of driving by practicing driving almost every day. It was now time to begin working on her fear of subways, which was right at the top of her hierarchy. This was important because Rachel needed to use the subway to get to work.

When it was suggested that Rachel ride the subway with her therapist, she initially refused. Because the subway was enclosed and escape was impossible (at least between stops), she was terrified that she would get stuck and would not be able to get out. Recognizing that people are often able to do more than they expect, her therapist suggested that they go to the subway platform and watch the trains go by for a while. Rachel was reassured that she would not have to get on the subway if she didn't feel ready to do so.

After about 15 minutes of watching the trains pass by, Rachel's therapist asked whether she might be willing to step on and off the subway car quickly, during the period that the doors were open. The therapist demonstrated this practice several times and then Rachel tried it when the next train arrived. She continued to step on and off each of the next three trains that stopped at the station. Next, Rachel's therapist asked whether she might be willing to go one stop on the subway. She was reassured that the stops were only about one minute apart, and her fear had decreased a bit, having seen a number of trains come and go. She decided to give it a try.

Rachel and her therapist traveled one stop and then got off the train. Having done it once and survived, Rachel agreed to try the same practice again. After a second successful try, Rachel agreed to ride the next train two stops with her therapist. She then agreed to ride the train for twenty minutes, sitting beside her therapist. Her fear level began at about an 80 out of 100, and gradually decreased to a moderate level (50) by the end of the twenty minutes.

At that point, Rachel felt ready to ride the train with her therapist sitting at the other end of the car. Again, her fear increased to about an 80 and then gradually decreased to a 50 after about ten minutes. Rachel and her therapist then returned to the therapist's office on separate subway cars. Although Rachel was exhausted, she was very pleased with her progress. At the start of the session, she was convinced that she would not be able to step foot on the train, but by the end of the session she was able to ride the train alone, with only a moderate level of discomfort. Over the next week, Rachel agreed to practice riding the subway daily with her husband.

Troubleshooting

Although exposure is usually a very effective way to reduce fear, the path is not always an easy one. In this section, we review some typical issues that may arise during exposure-based treatments, along with ways of solving each problem.

Problem: I don't fear or avoid specific situations. All my panic attacks occur out of the blue.

Solution: If your fears are not tied to specific situations, then there is no need for you to practice situational exposure. However, you may still benefit from symptom exposure (discussed in chapter 6) and from eliminating safety behaviors that you use to manage your anxiety (see chapter 7), as well as the other strategies reviewed in this book.

Problem: I'm too frightened to do my exposure practices.

Solution: If a particular exposure practice is too difficult, try something a bit easier. It is always better to practice something than to practice nothing at all. You may also want to identify a supportive person in your life who would be willing to help you practice a more difficult item. Often practicing with someone else will help reduce your fear to a point where you are then able to practice the item on your own.

Problem: My fear doesn't come down during my practices.

Solution: It is not unusual for people to have occasional practices with little reduction in fear, despite staying in the situation for a prolonged period. If your fear doesn't come down on a particular day, try again another day. However, if this is a consistent problem for you, it may be useful to examine what you are doing during your exposure practices. If you are ruminating about all the terrible things that might happen to you during a panic attack, try using the cognitive strategies discussed in chapter 4. Another factor that may interfere with fear reduction is excessive reliance on safety behaviors. As discussed in chapter 7, it's important to decrease your use of safety behaviors and other subtle forms of avoidance.

Problem: My fear returns between practices.

Solution: This is perfectly normal. Typically, people experience a reduction of fear during their exposure practices, but some of the fear returns between sessions, especially if there is a significant break between practices. Try to keep your practices close together. With repeated exposures, you will eventually notice less return of fear between practices.

Problem: I just can't seem to get myself to stay in the situation during my panic attacks.

Solution: As reviewed earlier, it is best to stay in the feared situation until your discomfort has decreased to a manageable level. If you're finding it difficult to stay in the situation when you feel panicky, there are a few ways of coping with the situation. First, you can do something to make the practices a bit easier. For example, you can initially use a few safety behaviors (for example, having another person with you), as long as you plan to do the practice at some later date without the safety behaviors. Alternatively, you can try a completely different practice—one that is easier and that you can stick with even if your anxiety gets high. If you must leave the situation, you can try to force yourself back into the situation once your anxiety has decreased. By leaving and re-entering feared situations over and over again, it may take a bit longer to overcome the fear, but the practices should still work over time. Finally, you may find it helpful to write down some helpful coping statements that you can say to yourself during the exposure to help you ride out your panic attack. Some examples include: "This panic attack will peak and then pass,"; "I will ride my panic like a wave,"; "The worst thing that will happen is I will feel uncomfortable,"; "I will feel very good when I complete this exposure practice,"; "I can cope with these uncomfortable physical sensations."

Problem: I can't seem to get around to practicing exposure. Things just seem to be too busy.

Solution: Try building the practices into your normal routine. For example, since you have to eat dinner anyway, try eating in a crowded restaurant, if that's one of the situations that bothers you. In addition to building practices into your normal routine, it is useful to schedule exposure practices the same way you would schedule any other appointment. You may even decide to cancel a few other activities or hire a baby sitter to make time for your exposure homework.

Problem: I worry that having a panic attack when driving is dangerous.

Solution: This is a common fear. We cannot guarantee that you won't get into a car accident during a panic attack. In fact, a high percentage of people without panic attacks get into minor car accidents from time to time. Still, the chances of a car accident during a panic attack are very small. Although it is true that panic symptoms may be distracting, there are lots of things that people do while driving that are distracting, including eating in the car, fiddling with the radio, talking on the phone, reading their mail, and putting on make-up. In all likelihood, a panic attack is no more distracting than these other activities. As long as you are an experienced driver with good safety habits (paying attention to the road, driving within the speed limit, not following too closely), chances are good that you will be safe. In fact, out of hundreds of people we have worked with who fear driving, none has ever had a car accident due to a panic attack. If you are concerned, you can always start your driving practices on less traveled roads, where the risk of an accident is reduced.

6

Confront Your Physical Symptoms

This chapter builds on the exposure strategies that you learned in chapter 5. In this chapter, you will learn about the role that fear of physical sensations plays in the maintenance of your panic disorder. You will identify the physical symptoms that make you feel anxious, and you will learn exposure strategies to confront the physical symptoms that you fear. With practice, you will find that your anxiety over physical symptoms is reduced and you'll feel more in control of your body.

The Role of Symptom Avoidance

Fear of the physical sensations of panic is at the heart of what maintains your panic disorder. Before you ever experienced panic attacks, you probably didn't pay close attention to your bodily sensations. However, after you experienced one or more unexpected panic attacks, bodily sensations may have taken on a new significance—they became associated with beliefs about danger. Once people make a connection between physical sensations and possible danger, they start to monitor their physical sensations as a way of preparing for potential danger and future panic. When those sensations are experienced, they trigger fear.

For example, Jeff was a successful businessman, married with two children and a busy social life. Jeff always felt appreciative of the successes he had experienced quite easily throughout his life. One day, Jeff was driving to work when, out of the blue, he experienced an intense rush of physical sensations. His heart pounded and he began to sweat and shake. He felt pain in his chest and was lightheaded. He drove straight to the emergency room at the hospital. He was sure that he was having a heart attack. At the hospital, Jeff was rushed in to see the doctor. A complete battery of tests was performed, and all findings were negative. There was nothing wrong with Jeff's heart. The doctor explained that Jeff's symptoms were caused by a panic attack.

Jeff found it difficult to believe that what he had experienced was a panic attack. He still felt that something could be wrong with his heart. He started to monitor his pulse throughout the day. Whenever he noticed his heart racing or pounding, his anxiety shot up and he experienced sensations similar to what he had experienced when he was driving. Jeff began to feel anxious about driving and about other situations, including flying, attending meetings out of town, eating in restaurants, and being in crowds. He also stopped going to the gym because exercise raised his heart rate and caused him to feel like he was going to have a panic attack.

This example clearly demonstrates how a fear of physical symptoms can cause you to avoid activities and situations that trigger the feared sensations. Just as exposure to feared situations can help you overcome situational fear and avoidance (as you learned in chapter 5), direct exposure to feared physical sensations will help you to overcome your fear of experiencing panic attacks and related symptoms. As you repeatedly practice bringing on the physical sensations that trigger your fear, your anxiety will decrease. You will feel less fearful of the sensations because you will learn that they simply aren't dangerous. You will also feel more in control when you experience physical sensations. You will learn that the worst thing that happens when you bring on intense physical sensations is that you feel uncomfortable. With repeated practice, you will start to view intense physical symptoms as a nuisance rather than as a sign of impending catastrophe.

Each person may fear different sensations, depending on the physical symptoms that are experienced during a panic attack. For Jeff, the physical symptom that he feared most was a racing or pounding heart. The first step in tackling your fear of physical symptoms is to identify the specific physical sensations that trigger your fear.

Exercise: Identify Your Feared Symptoms and Associated Beliefs

What physical sensations make you feel anxious or panicky? Think back to the last panic attack that you experienced. What was the first physical sensation that you noticed? What other physical sensations did you experience? What physical symptoms do you tend to monitor in your body (such as a racing heart, nausea or upset stomach, dizziness, feeling unreal, etc.)? Do you avoid any activities or substances because they might trigger physical sensations (for example, exercise, wearing a turtleneck, using the heater in your car, caffeine)? Thinking about the physical symptoms you fear, what potential catastrophes do you associate with these sensations (for example, dizziness = passing out, heart pounding = heart attack, nausea = vomiting, unreality = going crazy)? Record your responses to each of these questions in your journal.

Bringing on the Symptoms—Symptom Exposure

A variety of exercises have been developed to expose people to the sensations they fear. Before engaging in any of the suggested exercises, it is important to make sure that you don't have any medical conditions that would be aggravated by the exercise (for example, if you have asthma, you should skip over the hyperventilation exercise; or, if you have an ankle injury, you should skip jogging in place). Other medical conditions that might be aggravated by the symptom induction exercises include heart disease, migraines, and seizure disorders. If you are in doubt about the safety of a particular exercise, we recommend that you ask your family doctor for approval to engage in the symptom exposure practices.

When you engage in the symptom-induction exercises, the goal is to bring on the sensations so they are quite intense. If you feel overwhelmed, or if the sensations feel too strong, you may stop before the recommended time.

Exercise: Symptom Induction Testing

Before beginning the symptom-exposure exercises, it's important to discover which exercises are most effective for bringing on your feared symptoms. Below is a list of exercises for you to try. Immediately after you try each exercise, record the following information in your journal:

1. The physical sensations you experienced (the most commonly experienced symptoms are listed in parentheses after each exercise)

2. The intensity of your physical sensations, using a scale ranging from 0 (not at all) to 100 (extremely)

3. Your fear level, using a scale ranging from 0 (no fear) to 100 (the worst fear you can imagine)

4. The similarity of the physical sensations to those that you experience during a panic attack. Use a scale ranging from 0 (not at all similar) to 100 (extremely similar)

Here is the list of symptom-exposure exercises:

- Hyperventilate by breathing deeply and rapidly (about sixty to ninety breaths per minute), for sixty seconds (common symptoms include dizziness, breathlessness, racing heart, numbness, tingling).

- Breathe in and out through a small, narrow straw for two minutes. Do not breathe through your nose while you're doing the exercise, you may plug your nose if you like (breathlessness, racing heart, choking).

- Jog in place vigorously for two minutes (racing heart, breathlessness, chest discomfort).

- Spin in a chair for one minute (dizziness, racing heart, nausea).

- Stare at a light on the ceiling for one minute and then try and read (blurred vision).

- Shake your head from side to side for thirty seconds (dizziness).

- Hold your breath for thirty seconds or for as long as you can (breathlessness, dizziness).

- Place a tongue depressor on the back of your tongue for a few seconds or until you experience a gag reflex (choking feeling, gagging).

- Wear a turtleneck shirt, tie, or scarf (tightness in the throat).

- Stare at a dot on the wall (about the size of a dime) for three minutes (feeling of unreality).

- Sit in a hot stuffy room like a sauna or in your car with the heater on (hot, sweaty).

- Sit in a closet with your head covered by a coat for five minutes (breathlessness).

Once you've gone through the symptom testing, review the fear and similarity ratings you recorded for each exercise. Circle the three exercises that triggered the most anxiety for you and that were most similar to the physical sensations you experience during a panic attack. These three exercises will be your *target exercises*. We will refer back to these target exercises in the next section.

Exposure to Physical Symptoms

Now that you have identified some exercises that bring on anxiety provoking physical sensations, the next step in reducing your fear of physical symptoms is to practice the exercises repeatedly. With repeated practice, you will continue to experience similar sensations, but your fear of the sensations will decrease. As you practice symptom exposure, you will gradually weaken the association that was made during your early panic attacks between physical symptoms and danger.

The guidelines for conducting situational exposure (see chapter 5) apply to symptom exposure as well. Practices should be planned in advance, frequent (ideally, twice per day), and should last long enough to experience fear reduction. You should try not to engage in safety behaviors during the exposure practices (like making sure that you are not alone, keeping your medication handy). You should also practice challenging the anxious thoughts that arise as you engage in the exposure practice (see chapter 4).

Exercise: Confronting Scary Physical Sensations

Over the next week, choose one of your target exercises to practice. Set aside some time each day for your practices. At each practice, follow the steps below:

1. Complete your target symptom induction exercise to bring on feared physical sensations at high intensity

2. Immediately after engaging in the target exercise, answer the following questions and record your responses in your journal:

- What physical symptoms did you experience during, or immediately after engaging in the exercise?

- How intense were the physical sensations (using a 0 to 100 point scale, where 0 is not at all intense and 100 is extremely intense)?

- How high was your fear level during or after the practice (based on a 0 to 100 point scale, where "0" is not at all fearful and "100" is extremely fearful)?

- What anxious thoughts did you have in response to the physical sensations?

- What evidence do you have that supports or contradicts your anxious thoughts?

3. Wait a few minutes for the intensity of the physical sensations to reduce. Once your physical symptoms have reduced significantly, start over at step 1 and repeat your target exercise, then move on to steps 2 and 3. Repeat this cycle of steps until your initial fear level is reduced by about half. For example, if the first time you engage in your target exercise, you rate your fear at a 70, then you will repeat the exercise and these three steps until your fear is roughly a 35 or lower. This often requires repeating the exercise six or seven times.

It is useful to focus on just one target exercise until your fear is at a minimum before moving on to your other target exercises. It is recommended that you engage in symptom-exposure practices at least twice a day. The more you practice, the faster you will notice your fear decrease. Once you have tackled the first target exercise, move on to the second target exercise and repeat the process. When your fear of the symptoms triggered by the second target exercise is at a minimum, you are ready to move on to the third target exercise and repeat the steps above.

Remember that it's normal to feel anxious about engaging in symptom exposure. You may be thinking to yourself, "Why would I want to bring on my panic sensations when what I'm trying to do is get rid of them! These exercises seem crazy." In order to tackle your anxiety around physical symptoms, it is useful to experience the symptoms repeatedly, in a controlled manner. It will be difficult to recover from panic disorder if you continue to fear and avoid physical symptoms, because it is the fear of physical sensations that keeps the problem alive. As you confront the sensations you fear, your anxiety will decrease and you will feel more in control of your body. When you reach a point at which physical symptoms are no longer anxiety provoking, you will have conquered your panic disorder.

If you suffer from a medical condition that causes physical symptoms such as vertigo (dizziness), diabetes (shakiness, palpitations, etc.), or asthma (shortness of breath, breathing difficulties) it can be helpful to try and monitor your symptoms in an effort to distinguish between symptoms caused by your medical condition and those caused by panic. At first it may be difficult to tease them apart. It is our experience that as people continue monitoring their symptoms, they eventually become better able to distinguish panic symptoms from medical symptoms. This is important because symptoms of a true medical condition may be signals that you need to respond in some way (for example, taking insulin in response to high blood sugar in diabetes, using an inhaler in response to asthma). However, if the physical symptoms are due to panic, then it's important that you do not respond to them in ways that help to maintain your fear.

Confronting Activities that Trigger Symptoms

Just as you may avoid situations that are associated with panic, you may also avoid certain activities that bring on scary physical sensations. Recall that Jeff, who we met earlier in the chapter, avoided going to the gym because exercising caused his heart rate to increase, triggering his concerns that he might have a heart attack. Common activities that people may avoid because they bring on physical sensations include:

- Going to the gym
- Participating in sports (for example, a hockey or soccer game)
- Running or jogging
- Going for a brisk walk
- Hiking
- Consuming caffeine (such as tea, coffee, soda, chocolate)
- Drinking hot beverages
- Wearing constricting or warm clothing (like a turtleneck, tie, heavy sweater)
- Watching action films or scary movies
- Walking up stairs
- Going out when you are not feeling 100 percent well

- Only engaging in the activities listed above when you're with a safe person (not alone) or when using safety behaviors (like carrying a cell phone, medication, repeatedly checking for symptoms, engaging in reassurance seeking)

Avoiding activities that bring on or intensify physical symptoms helps to maintain your fear of symptoms, making it more likely that you will continue to experience panic attacks. In the same way that you gradually confronted feared situations in chapter 5, it is important to also gradually confront activities that produce uncomfortable physical symptoms.

Exercise: Confront Physical Activities

In your journal, make a list of the activities that you fear or avoid because of the physical symptoms they produce. Think about any safety behaviors that you may use to help you manage these activities and include them in your list. Use the same steps that you followed in chapter 5 to construct an exposure hierarchy of the physical activities you fear or avoid. Beside each entry, record your typical level of fear when engaging in the activity, with or without your safety behavior, using a scale ranging from 0 (no fear; never avoid) to 100 (as frightened as you can imagine being; would avoid the activity at almost any cost).

As an example, Jeff's activity hierarchy is listed below.

Activity	Fear Rating
Go to the gym alone without my cell phone	100
Continue what I am doing when my heart is racing (don't sit down)	90
Go for a run around the block alone	85
Go to the gym alone with my cell phone	75
Run up the stairs in my house	70
Run around the block with a friend	65
Have an espresso coffee in the morning on my way to work	55
Don't check my pulse when I notice my heart racing	50
Go to the gym with a friend	45

Once you have constructed your activity hierarchy, you can use the same steps that you learned in chapter 5 to practice exposure. Remember the following principles:

- Select activities that trigger at least a moderate level of fear.

- Practice each activity for an extended period, at least a few times per week, for a period of a few weeks or months (or until it is no longer frightening).

- Plan your practices in advance so they are predictable, controlled, and frequent.

- Monitor your fear level throughout the practice (using a 0 to 100 point scale).

- Make sure your practices are long enough to experience a significant reduction in fear.

- Do not engage in safety behaviors (for example, checking your pulse or distraction).

- Practice countering your anxious thoughts during exposures using the techniques you learned in chapter 4.

Combine Symptom Exposure with Situational Exposure

Now that you have practiced symptom exposure and tackled activities that trigger physical symptoms, the final step is to combine symptom exposure with exposure to the situations that you practiced in chapter 5. Combining symptom exposure with situational exposure will teach you that not only is it okay to experience the sensations you fear in relatively safe situations (such as home), but it is even okay to experience these symptoms in the situations you fear.

The guidelines for combining situational exposure and symptom exposure are similar to those for other types of exposure (as reviewed in chapter 5). For example, Jeff combined exercises to increase his heart rate with going to a crowded shopping mall. He jogged from his car in the parking lot to the mall entrance (watching out for cars, of course!). He ran up and down the steps in the mall, and then walked around the mall at a brisk pace at intervals to increase his heart rate. At first, his fear was quite high (80), but as he continued to practice, his fear decreased to a minimal level (40).

Exercise: Confront Your Feared Symptoms and Situations Together

Review the situational exposure hierarchy that you constructed in chapter 5. Make a list of five to ten practices that combine situational exposure with one of the target symptom exposure exercises that you identified and practiced in this chapter. You can also include other exercises that are likely to trigger the physical symptoms that make you anxious. Over the next few weeks, practice the items on your combined list using the recommended exposure guidelines. Remember, the more you practice, the faster you will see results.

Stop Playing it Safe—Eliminating Subtle Avoidance

In chapters 5 and 6 you began to confront feared situations and sensations through direct exposure. Exposure is one of the most powerful methods of reducing fear because it teaches you that the outcomes and consequences so often anticipated during panic attacks almost never come true. However, for many individuals, exposure to feared situations is undermined by subtle forms of avoidance and overreliance on various safety behaviors. In other words, people often use "safety nets" when confronting feared situations, just in case something bad happens.

The use of safety behaviors helps to keep your fear under control. That's why these strategies are used so frequently. However, these behaviors also prevent you from learning that the situations and symptoms you fear are in fact perfectly safe. For example, if every time you feel panicky you sit down to prevent your heart rate from getting too high, you may be left with the impression that the only reason you have survived each time is because you sat down. Ideally, it's important to learn that a panic attack is perfectly safe whether you are sitting down, walking around, or standing on your head. The purpose of this chapter is to help you to identify your own most frequently used safety behaviors and to develop a plan to eliminate them so that your exposure practices have the maximum impact.

Common Safety Behaviors

Below is a list of safety behaviors and subtle avoidance strategies that are sometimes used by individuals who suffer from panic attacks and panic disorder. As you review the list, consider whether you sometimes use some of these strategies and whether there are other ways that you try to manage your anxiety that are not listed here.

CARRYING SAFETY OBJECTS. In order to control anxiety and fear, people with panic disorder often carry various objects that help them to feel safer. For example, they may carry around their medication, even if they have no intention of taking it. We have also seen individuals who carry around a drink (for example, a bottle of water) or hard candy in case their throat gets dry. Some people feel uncomfortable unless they have various self-help books with them, perhaps with key passages highlighted. Some people also carry money (to make an emergency phone call), a mobile phone, a paper bag (in case they hyperventilate or need to throw up), and even a blood-pressure monitor.

DISTRACTION. Distraction is a common method used to manage feelings of anxiety. If people can't avoid a situation physically, they often try to avoid it mentally. Examples of distraction include imagining being somewhere else, focusing on anything but your physical symptoms, talking to the person next to you on a plane or in the car, reading a book, frantically doing housework, watching television, singing a song in your head, or listening to a portable stereo. Generally, there is nothing wrong with reading a book, talking to other people, or doing housework. These behaviors are only problematic when they are used in a desperate attempt to avoid experiencing feared panic sensations. As with all safety behaviors, distraction prevents you from learning that periods of anxiety and fear are not dangerous.

SEEKING REASSURANCE. When you feel anxious or panicky, do you ask for reassurance from others to make sure that you are not in fact dying, going crazy, or about to lose control? We all like to feel reassured. However, when asking for reassurance becomes a habit, it can undermine your ability to overcome panic attacks on your own. It can also place a strain on your relationships.

CHECKING BEHAVIORS. Checking your pulse, breathing rate, or blood pressure are just other examples of reassurance seeking. The truth is that if you are physically healthy, it doesn't matter what your body does during your panic attacks. There is no need to check. Checking behaviors just serves to fuel anxiety and increase your focus on the body.

BEING ACCOMPANIED. A need to be accompanied by a safe person is a hallmark feature of panic disorder and agoraphobia. More often than not, people with this problem feel safer when they are with a spouse, family member, or close friend. They may even require a particular safe person (like a spouse or parent) to carry a pager or mobile phone so they can be reached at all times. This increased dependency on others undermines your independence and erodes your self-confidence. When overcoming panic attacks, gradually spending more time alone despite any initial increases in anxiety and panic will be useful.

STAYING NEAR EXITS. People who experience panic attacks often feel safer if they are sitting near the exit on a bus or subway, in a restaurant, or in a theater. They may also insist on sitting in an aisle seat when seeing a movie or play or attending a lecture. When driving on highways, they may feel more comfortable in the right lane than in the left lane. Being near the exits makes you feel safer because escape is easier in the event of a panic attack. Of course, as reviewed in chapter 4, a helpful question to be asking yourself is "Why do I need to escape? So what if I have a panic attack in the situation?" Staying near exits prevents you from really challenging your fears head on.

BREATHING INTO A PAPER BAG. Some people breathe into a paper bag when they feel anxious or panicky. Although this strategy may seem to help in the short term, there are no studies to answer the question of whether this strategy actually makes a difference (the belief that your anxiety will decrease may be enough to cause actual decreases in symptoms). Regardless, in the long term it is probably not useful because it's just another form of avoidance. To learn that your symptoms are not dangerous, it is important to stop finding subtle ways to avoid them.

USING ALCOHOL OR DRUGS TO MANAGE ANXIETY. It's not surprising that people use alcohol to cope with feelings of anxiety. In fact, alcohol acts on the same brain chemicals as many anti-anxiety medications, in particular the benzodiazepines (see chapter 10). Other drugs (both legal and illegal) may also reduce anxiety in the short term. However, be aware that drugs that reduce anxiety now may lead to withdrawal symptoms later. This is certainly the case with alcohol. Although drinking alcohol may lower your anxiety levels initially, a few hours later you will be more likely to panic than if you'd drunk nothing. In addition, overreliance on alcohol and drugs will prevent you from learning that it's perfectly safe to experience your anxiety symptoms. Instead of helping you to overcome your panic, reliance on alcohol or drugs just creates another problem in your life.

CONTROLLING THE ENVIRONMENT. People with panic disorder sometimes make changes to their surroundings as a way of controlling their panic symptoms. For example, they may insist on having the door open in the bathroom or when seeing a family doctor. Or, they may keep the window open in the car (for fresh air) or avoid using the heater. People who are susceptible to panicking while lying in bed sometimes leave the lights or television on when going to sleep (as a distraction). Or they may stay up very late to make sure that they feel tired. This ensures they fall asleep more quickly and thereby avoid experiencing anxiety symptoms.

Exercise: Identify Your Safety Behaviors

In your journal, make a list of strategies that you use to manage your anxiety. You can choose from the safety behaviors reviewed in this chapter or from others that you can think of. Think about how anxious you would be to give up these behaviors. If the thought of giving up a particular subtle avoidance strategy is anxiety provoking, chances are that this is a behavior that you will eventually want to eliminate as you work toward overcoming your panic attacks.

Eliminating Subtle Avoidance and Safety Behaviors

Now that you have identified the subtle avoidance behaviors that you use, it's time to begin eliminating them. This can be done gradually and can be built into the exposure practices that you are already doing. For example, if you have been practicing driving on highways but have been careful to always stay in the right lane, a natural next step might be to begin driving in the left lane. Similarly, if you always carry certain items with you during exposure practices (for example, your medication), try leaving these items with someone else or at home the next time you practice exposure.

Exercise: Reducing Safety Behaviors

If you have continued to use certain safety behaviors during exposure practices or at other times, try to gradually reduce these behaviors over the next few weeks. In your journal, record your fear level during each practice, using a scale ranging from 0 (no fear) to 100 (maximum fear), as well as any anxious thoughts that arise. Continue to use the cognitive strategies discussed in chapter 4 to challenge any anxious beliefs that occur.

Learn to Breathe Normally

Hyperventilation occurs when you breathe too quickly for your body's needs. It's not unusual for people to occasionally hyperventilate or overbreathe, particularly when they are under stress or feeling frightened. Although hyperventilation is not dangerous, it can lead to uncomfortable physical sensations. As you will recall from practicing the hyperventilation exercise in chapter 6, overbreathing can bring on a number of the most common panic symptoms, including light-headedness, dizziness, numbness and tingling sensations, chest tightness, sweating, feelings of unreality, and shortness of breath. These symptoms are caused by a drop in the carbon dioxide level in your blood that occurs when your body takes in more oxygen than you need. In addition to being triggered by intense emotions, hyperventilation can sometimes be a habit. In other words, some people normally breathe at a slightly higher rate than necessary, which can make them more prone to experiencing certain uncomfortable symptoms, especially if they sigh or take a deep breath.

The Role of Hyperventilation in Panic Disorder

The role of breathing in maintaining panic disorder is complex. There is some evidence that breathing irregularities may play a role in maintaining panic disorder for some people (Abelson et al. 2001). For example, one study found that individuals with panic disorder tended to breathe more quickly compared to individuals with another anxiety disorder or people without an anxiety disorder (Munjack, Brown, and McDowell 1993). However, other researchers (for example, Taylor 2001) have concluded that hyperventilation does not play a major role in triggering panic attacks.

It's possible that a subgroup of people with panic disorder are more prone to hyperventilation (Moynihan and Gevirtz 2001). For these people, learning how to normalize their breathing (also called *breathing retraining*) may be a useful component of treatment. The breathing retraining strategy covered in this chapter is based on procedures described by Rapee (1985) and later by Craske and Barlow (2001).

Do you have a tendency to hyperventilate? Complete the exercise below to determine whether breathing retraining would be a beneficial strategy for you.

Exercise: Assess Your Breathing

Ask someone else to count your breaths (for example, by watching your chest) for a period of one minute (ideally at a time when you don't know they are counting, because your breathing rate may change if you start to pay attention to it). Record this number in your journal. The normal breathing rate at rest ranges from ten to fourteen breaths per minute. If your breathing rate was higher than this range, you may benefit from the breathing retraining methods reviewed in this chapter.

Now, take a few minutes to pay attention to your breathing. What part of your chest moves when you inhale? If your upper chest moves out when you breathe in, you may be more prone to hyperventilation (when people breathe too quickly, they often use their upper chest muscles to breathe rather than their diaphragm). If your abdomen moves out most when you inhale, you may already be breathing properly, and the techniques described in this chapter may be less useful for you.

If you are having trouble telling whether you are breathing from your upper chest or abdomen, here are some strategies to help you out. Place one hand on your chest, with your thumb just below your neck. Place your other hand on your abdomen, with your baby finger just above your belly button. Now try to breathe normally. Do you feel one hand moving more than the other as your inhale and exhale? For the next minute, try to move your chest in and out when you breathe. Does your breathing change when you try to breathe from your chest? Record your responses in your journal. Next, try to move your abdomen in and out as you breathe. Do this for about a minute. How does your breathing change when you try to breathe from your abdomen? Record your responses in your journal.

You probably noticed that when you breathed from your chest you took more shallow breaths, with more breaths per minute than when you breathed from your abdomen. This exercise demonstrates nicely how chest breathing can lead to hyperventilation symptoms, even when you're not even aware of it. It may seem like the symptoms are coming out of the blue, even though they are really being caused by over-breathing. In contrast, you probably noticed that when you breathed from your abdomen, your breathing was slower and more relaxed. Learning to breathe from your abdomen, using your diaphragm muscle, is the goal of breathing retraining. These strategies are similar to the type of breathing used by professional singers, individuals who study yoga, and others for whom proper breathing is essential.

Breathing Retraining

Although breathing retraining may be useful for you to try, research has shown that it is not an essential component in treatment for panic disorder (Schmidt et al. 2000). In fact, in some ways, breathing retraining may interfere with your use of the cognitive and behavioral strategies you developed thus far. This can happen when people use breathing retraining in a desperate attempt to distract themselves, escape, or avoid experiencing panic symptoms. When this happens, breathing retraining may prevent you from learning that your feared predictions don't come true during a panic attack. Though it is perfectly fine to use breathing retraining as a general strategy to relax or to reduce symptoms of hyperventilation, it should not be used as a safety behavior, to protect you from symptoms that you perceive as dangerous. To overcome fear, the exposure-based strategies and cognitive techniques described earlier in this book should be viewed as the core strategies. Breathing retraining should be viewed as a secondary strategy that may be useful, particularly for individuals who tend to hyperventilate.

Exercise: Normalizing Your Breathing

The goal of breathing retraining is to teach you to breathe from your diaphragm, at a slower, more relaxed pace. Slow breathing should not to be confused with *deep* breathing, which may actually cause you to hyperventilate (if you have ever blown up a beach ball or a bunch of balloons, you know that breathing too deeply and too quickly can cause dizziness and other symptoms). Breath through your nose if possible. If you have bad allergies or a cold this may be more difficult.

Step 1: Breathe from your diaphragm. Place one hand on your chest with your thumb just below your neck. Place your other hand on your abdomen, with your baby finger just above your belly button. Practice breathing from your diaphragm so that as you inhale, your abdomen moves slightly outward. Continue breathing this way until you can do this comfortably. If you have difficulty doing this sitting up, you may find it easier at first to practice while lying on your back.

As you practice the exercise, count to yourself each time you *inhale*. When you reach 10, go back to 1 and start your counting over again. Each time you *exhale*, mentally repeat the word "relax." So, your thoughts should be focused on repeating to yourself "1-relax; 2-relax; 3-relax; 4-relax; 5-relax; 6-relax; 7-relax; 8-relax; 9-relax; 10-relax." When you exhale and mentally tell yourself to relax, try to imagine yourself becoming more relaxed.

For the next week, practice breathing through your nose, using your diaphragm muscle (abdominal breathing) and including the counting and relaxation exercises. You should practice for 10 minutes at a time at least twice per day. At this stage, try to keep your rate of breathing normal. Don't slow it down yet. For now, use the exercises in situations that are not anxiety provoking (for example, in a quiet room at home when you are feeling calm).

Step 2: Slowing down your breathing. After practicing the exercise for one week at your normal rate of breathing, the next step is to slow your breathing down to a more relaxed pace. Ideally, this should be three seconds for each inhale and three seconds for each exhale. One way of doing this is to count to 3 as you inhale and again as you exhale. You should also remember to count to 10 on the inhales and to repeat the word "relax" on the exhales. Essentially, you should be counting as in step 1, combined with counting the number of seconds in each inhale and exhale cycle. It's a bit complicated, so let's run though what you would actually be saying to yourself:

First inhalation/exhalation cycle:
"1-2-3; relax-2-3"

Second inhalation/exhalation cycle:
"2-2-3; relax-2-3"

Third inhalation/exhalation cycle: "3-2-3;
relax-2-3"

Fourth inhalation/exhalation cycle:
"4-2-3; relax-2-3"

Fifth inhalation/exhalation cycle:
"5-2-3; relax-2-3"

Sixth inhalation/exhalation cycle:
"6-2-3; relax-2-3"

Seventh inhalation/exhalation cycle:
"7-2-3; relax-2-3"

Eighth inhalation/exhalation cycle:
"8-2-3; relax-2-3"

Ninth inhalation/exhalation cycle:
"9-2-3; relax-2-3"

Tenth inhalation/exhalation cycle:
"10-2-3; relax-2-3"

After you reach the tenth cycle, go back to "1-2-3; relax-2-3" and start counting to 10 all over again. For the next week, continue to practice your slow breathing for ten minutes at a time at least twice per day. For now, continue to use the exercises in a quiet, relaxed setting.

Step 3: Practicing in anxiety provoking situations. As you become more comfortable using the breathing exercise, you can start to practice it when you are feeling more anxious, or when you are in anxiety provoking situations. In your journal, record your anxiety level (0 to 100 point scale) before and after using the breathing retraining exercises. Remember, breathing retraining is a tool for reducing levels of general anxiety and stress. It should not be used in desperation to protect you from experiencing feared symptoms.

Troubleshooting

A number of challenges may arise while trying to use the breathing retraining strategies. Some of the most common ones are listed below, along with solutions.

Problem: Distracting thoughts enter my head, making it hard to concentrate while doing my exercises.

Solution: As you practice breathing, try to focus on counting your breaths (counting up to 10). If you find that other thoughts pop into your head, that's okay. Acknowledge the thought and then refocus your attention back to your breathing and counting. Simply return to 1 and start your counting again. Breathing in this way is a skill that takes practice. As you continue to practice, you'll find it easier to turn your attention back to your breathing when thoughts come into your mind.

Problem: The three-second pace is difficult to maintain.

Solution: For some people, three seconds is not long enough for either the inhalation or exhalation. If three seconds feels too short, try increasing each inhalation and exhalation to four seconds. If you find the counting difficult or distracting, try instead to focus on slowing down your breathing and on mentally repeating the word "relax" during each exhale. Forget about the counting for a week or so. Once you have become more comfortable taking longer breaths, you can try to count again and it will probably be easier. Remember, breathing in this way is a skill that takes time and practice to develop. It's not something that you can master immediately, particularly if your natural tendency has been to overbreathe.

Problem: Breathing retraining triggers anxiety.

Solution: It's normal to experience some anxiety when engaging in the breathing exercise. It is not surprising that an exercise that has you focus on your body may trigger some anxiety. If this happens, just ride it through and continue to practice. As you become more comfortable using the exercise, you will feel less anxious.

Reduce Life Stress and Improve Your Health

Stress is something that we are all exposed to—it's a part of living. Stressors can range from significant life events (like the death of someone close to you, losing or changing jobs, switching schools, having a new baby, moving, getting married or divorced, etc.) to minor, everyday hassles (for example, running late for an appointment, having no time for yourself, having too much to do, or arguing with your significant other). In fact, almost any change, whether it is positive or negative, can be a source of stress.

Stress can play an important role in the development and maintenance of panic disorder. Many of our patients have reported that their panic attacks first began during or just after a stressful period in their lives. In addition, there is some evidence to suggest that people with panic disorder may be more sensitive to the effects of stress than people without panic disorder. One study found that people with panic disorder had greater changes in their heart rate in response to everyday life events (a measure of the way people respond to stress) than did individuals without any anxiety or other psychological problems

(Anastasiades et al. 1990). There is also evidence that ongoing stressful life events can interfere with recovery from panic disorder (Wade, Monroe, and Michelson 1993).

Exercise: Identify Your Sources of Stress—Past and Current

The purpose of this exercise is to help you understand the relationship between stress and your experience of panic, both past and current. Record your responses to the following questions in your journal.

Past. Although we cannot change the past, it can be helpful to understand the role that stress may have played in the onset of your panic attacks. Think back to when your panic attacks first began. What was going on in your life at the time? What stressors (major or minor) were you experiencing? Is there a connection between the stress you were under and the development of your panic attacks?

Current. Now consider the past year. Did you experience any stress, changes, or difficulties in any of the following areas: family, personal relationships, your physical health, the physical health of significant others, finances, legal problems, work, or school? Did you experience any major stresses in the past year that aren't covered by these categories? Now consider your everyday life in the past week. What sort of daily hassles or ongoing stresses have you experienced? What issues have been sources of stress for you? What problems have you had to cope with? How is your anxiety and panic affected by changes in your stress level?

Strategies for General Stress Reduction

Now that you have a better understanding of your current stresses and the impact stress has on your panic, you are in a better position to reduce stress and develop stress-management strategies. There are a number of different ways to manage stress in your life. The rest of this chapter reviews strategies that may be useful for reducing the effects of stress. For a more detailed discussion of these and other stress-reduction methods, there are a number of excellent books available. Two of these include *The Unofficial Guide to Beating Stress* (Goudey 2000) and the *Relaxation and Stress Reduction Workbook* (Davis, Eshelman, and McKay 2000).

REDUCE SOURCES OF STRESS

This strategy often seems easier than it really is. It may be hard to say "no" to requests on your time, or you may find it challenging to limit how much you take on. Consider the sources of stress that you identified in the last exercise. Can you think of ways that you can eliminate some of these sources? If you cannot eliminate a source of stress completely, consider the ways that you can reduce its effect on your life (for example, sharing responsibility, asking for help, etc.).

PROBLEM SOLVING

Day-to-day problems are a common source of stress for most of us. In fact, sometimes there are so many problems in a person's life that it seems impossible to decide which one to tackle first. Problem solving is a strategy that has been shown to be effective for reducing the effects of stress. As you start to solve the problems in your life one by one, you will feel more effective and in control. Problem solving is a skill that you can develop by following the steps below. These steps are based on problem-solving techniques outlined by Mynors-Wallis and Hegel (2000).

1. **Make a problem list.** Include all of the problems that are affecting you in your life. Consider the following areas: your relationship with a partner, relationships with family members and friends, finances, health, work or school, housing, legal issues, and any other area of functioning.

2. **Select one problem to work on.** Although your problem list may look a bit overwhelming, tackling problems one at a time will make the process much more manageable. Choose the problem that you want to work on first. This may be the problem that is bothering you the most, or perhaps a problem that is most easily solved.

3. **Set a goal.** If the problem you identified was solved, how would your life be different? What would you be doing differently? What would you like to see change? Use your answers to these questions to set a goal for yourself in relation to the problem you are working on. Your goal should be specific, realistic, and achievable.

4. **Brainstorm.** Take some time to consider all the possible strategies or solutions for achieving your goal. Write each strategy down without evaluating or judging whether it is useful.

5. **Select a solution.** Consider the list of possible solutions that you generated. Choose one solution to try first. If you find it difficult to select a solution, try writing down the costs and benefits of implementing each solution.

6. **Make a plan.** What steps will you take to carry out your solution? Write these steps down.

7. **Implement your plan.** Put your plan into action.

8. **Evaluate the outcome.** How did your solution work out? If you were successful in achieving your goal, you can set another goal to continue working on the problem you selected (going back to step 3), or you can choose another problem to work on and begin the process back at step 1. If you did not achieve your goal, what obstacles got in the way? Consider revising your plan (step 6) or choosing another solution (step 5).

TIME MANAGEMENT

Another strategy for alleviating stress is to manage time more effectively. Try using a day planner or diary to schedule what you need to do on a daily basis. Don't forget to schedule time for yourself every day. Once you have scheduled your time, it will become clearer whether the demands on your time are realistic or whether you need to reduce them.

RELAXATION

Relaxation techniques are another effective method for reducing the effects of stress. Specifically, relaxation exercises decrease levels of overarousal in the body—a common side effect of stress. There are various ways to incorporate relaxation into your life:

- Use the breathing exercise from chapter 8.

- Join a yoga or meditation class.

- Listen to a relaxation tape.

Try to incorporate time for relaxation *every* day.

GETTING SOCIAL SUPPORT

Often, the effects of stress are magnified when you have less social supports in place and you feel you are managing things on your own. Increasing your social support network is a very helpful strategy for reducing stress. Consider the following options and determine what might work best for you:

- Talk to your family about ways in which they may be able to help.

- Talk to friends.

- Find out about different resources that might be available in your community (like support groups, financial aid services, community center programs).

- Consider seeing a private therapist (psychologist, psychiatrist, social worker).

- Talk to your family doctor.

- If religion is an important part of your life, you can approach your priest, rabbi, or spiritual leader for guidance.

Exercise: Develop A Stress-Management Plan

Consider the different strategies that we discussed to help reduce your stress. For each source of stress that you identified in the last exercise, indicate how you will use these strategies to manage your stress. Record your plan in your journal.

IMPROVING HEALTH HABITS

Poor health habits can also make it more difficult to cope with stress and can exacerbate anxiety. Focusing on improving your health habits involves making sure your nutritional needs are met, ensuring you have good sleep habits, and incorporating physical activity in your life.

Eating Right

Anxiety can lead to reduced appetite and missed meals. Alternatively, some people eat more during times of anxiety. If your body's nutritional needs are not met, you will experience fatigue and low energy. Such a state will leave you with fewer resources to cope with stress, thereby increasing your levels of anxiety. Your goal should be to have three nutritionally balanced meals per day and, if needed, one or two snacks.

Getting a Good Night's Sleep

People often tell us that their anxiety was heightened when they didn't get enough sleep the previous night. Lack of sleep may contribute to feeling overly emotional and unable to cope. You should aim to have seven to eight hours of sleep per night, although different amounts of sleep are required at different ages (for example, we need less sleep as we get older). It is also good to have a sleep routine where you try to go to bed and get up around the same time each day. If you are having difficulties sleeping, it's a good idea to discuss the problems with your family doctor. An excellent book that discusses proven strategies for overcoming insomnia is *No More Sleepless Nights* by Peter Hauri and Shirley Linde (1996).

Incorporating Exercise

As you will remember from chapter 6, people with panic disorder often avoid exercise because it brings on unpleasant physical symptoms that are associated with anxiety. To fully recover from panic and to focus on improving your overall health and well-being, it is useful to incorporate exercise into your life. Exercise has both physical and emotional benefits and will help you to feel better about yourself. In fact, some researchers have found that exercise alone is effective for specifically reducing symptoms of panic disorder (Broocks et al. 1998). Try to incorporate at least twenty minutes of physical activity three to four times per week.

Exercise: Focusing on Your
Health Habits

Consider your health habits—your nutrition, sleep, and activity level. What areas of your health would benefit from improvement? What goals do you want to set for these areas? What steps will you take to achieve your goals? What obstacles are in your way? How will you overcome these obstacles? What sources of support can you use? Record your responses in your journal.

IMPROVING YOUR RELATIONSHIPS

You might be surprised to learn that your relationships can contribute to your panic attacks and also may interfere with recovery, particularly in the case of severe agoraphobia (Carter, Turovsky, and Barlow 1994). As people recover from panic disorder, particularly with agoraphobia, they become more independent and less reliant on family members for support and assistance. This can be threatening for family members and can lead to conflict or stress in relationships.

For example, Betty had panic disorder and agoraphobia for twenty years before she received help at our clinic. When Betty first began treatment, her husband did everything for her and for the household. He drove Betty everywhere. He did all of the shopping. He also accompanied Betty to appointments and social events, when she would go. Betty even found it difficult to walk further than the end of her street unaccompanied by her husband, because of her fear of panic symptoms. Over the years, Betty's husband had responded to her anxiety by making things easier for her and by taking on more of the responsibility in the house. When family members try to reduce a loved one's symptoms by taking on the individual's responsibilities or activities, we call this *symptom accommodation.*

Over the course of treatment, Betty began to try all of the things that she had stopped doing twenty years ago (like driving, going to the store alone, going to social events alone, etc.). These changes were disruptive for the life that Betty and her husband had lived for so many years. Initially, it caused some stress on their marriage as Betty's husband had to adjust to changes in Betty and their lifestyle. If Betty's husband had been less understanding, it may have been more difficult for her to recover from panic disorder as recovery required her husband to give back some control over the relationship.

Exercise: Panic Disorder and Your Relationships

Think about your immediate family relationships. Has your panic disorder had an impact on these relationships? How has anxiety affected your relationships? Are there roles and responsibilities that you gave up because of your panic? What are the ways that your family members may be accommodating your panic symptoms?

If you identified that your relationships have been affected by your panic disorder, then it is also possible that they will be affected by your recovery. It's a good idea to educate your partner or family members about the recovery process and the changes that may take place as you become more confident and less dependent. It is helpful to let them know that your new independence isn't a reflection on them but rather an important part of the process of overcoming your panic disorder.

10 Choose Medications that Work

Throughout this book, we have emphasized cognitive and behavioral approaches to managing your panic and anxiety. However, psychological treatment is not the only approach that has been shown to be effective. Medication can also be useful. In fact, cognitive behavioral therapy (CBT) and medications are generally found to be about equally effective, particularly in the short term (for a review, see Antony and Swinson 2000). This chapter reviews issues related to the use of medications for panic disorder, outlines the major medication options, and summarizes what we know about the relative effects of medications and combinations of CBT and medication, both in the short term and the long term.

As we discuss the medications used for treating panic, we will mention whether the evidence is based on placebo-controlled trials versus uncontrolled studies, which simply examine changes in anxiety after treatment compared to before treatment. Placebo-controlled trials are designed to examine the effects of a medication compared to the effects of taking an inactive placebo (a pill that contains no real medication). There is lots of evidence that simply taking a pill, even if it contains no real medication, can lead to a reduction in anxiety and panic for more than a third of individuals. In other words, an uncontrolled study showing that a medication leads to a reduction in anxiety is not all that impressive. For a drug to be considered effective, it must be shown to have panic-reducing properties over and above the effects of placebo or comparable to another effective medication.

This chapter provides a basic overview of the medications used to treat panic disorder. For those interested in more detailed information on the medications discussed in this book, a number of other resources are available (Bezchlibnyk-Butler and Jeffries 2004; Fuller and Sajatovic 2001; Roy-Byrne and Cowley 2002; Russo 2001; Sifton 2002).

Should You Consider Taking Medications?

The decision about whether to take medication for your panic attacks is one that should be made in consultation with your family doctor or a psychiatrist. Many different factors should be considered in this decision, including:

- Your preference for trying medication versus a different approach (such as CBT). If you don't want to take medications, you don't have to. Other options are available

- Whether you're already taking other medications that may interact with the drug you are considering for panic

- Your previous response to medications for panic

- The availability of various treatment options in your community (for example, if there are no CBT practitioners where you live, medication may be your best option)

- Your sensitivity to the side effects of medication

- Whether you have a medical condition that may interact with the medication

- Whether you are pregnant or breastfeeding your baby (though keep in mind that there are no known risks associated with taking many of the medications used to treat panic disorder while pregnant or breast feeding)

- Whether you use drugs or alcohol that may interact with your medication

People with panic disorder are sometimes apprehensive about taking medications, often because of misinformation or exaggerated fears. Some individuals are frightened of taking a foreign substance into their bodies that may induce panic sensations or trigger a panic attack. Others are apprehensive about swallowing pills for fear that it will trigger a choking or gagging response. People may also believe that having to take medication for a problem like panic disorder is a sign of failure or weakness, and they may avoid taking medications due to the perceived stigma or embarrassment associated with these treatments.

Be reassured that for the majority of individuals who take the medications described in this chapter, the benefits outweigh the costs. Although drugs used to treat panic attacks can cause side effects, these symptoms are manageable for most people, they often decrease over time, and they can be minimized by starting at a low dosage and increasing the dosage very slowly. Furthermore, in our experience, the stigma that was once associated with these products is much less now. Millions of people take these medications. In fact, the drugs described in this chapter are among the most commonly prescribed medications on the market. Finally, you probably have little to lose by trying medication. If it doesn't work out, you can always stop the medication, try a different drug, try a psychological treatment, or try no treatment at all. The decision to try medication is unlikely to have any permanent or long-term effects.

ADVANTAGES AND DISADVANTAGES OF MEDICATION TREATMENT

The main advantage of treatment with medication is that it works. Most of the medications that we discuss in the chapter have been clinically proven to block panic attacks and reduce levels of anxiety, compared to treatment with placebo. In addition, compared to CBT, medications are easy to use, easy to obtain, quick to begin working, and less expensive, at least in the short term.

However, in the long term, medications may be more expensive than CBT, and the effects don't last as long once treatment has stopped. In most studies comparing CBT to medication treatments for panic disorder, the effects of CBT tend to be longer lasting than the effects of medication. Rates of relapse tend to be higher upon stopping medication (though some individuals are able to stop taking their medications without experiencing a recurrence of symptoms). Other disadvantages of medications include side effects; interactions with other medications, drugs, and alcohol; possible effects on preexisting medical conditions (for example, increasing the likelihood of seizures or elevated blood pressure); and withdrawal symptoms upon stopping treatment. Because of these possible problems, the products described in this chapter should only be started or discontinued under the supervision of a doctor.

Antidepressants for Panic Disorder

Don't be fooled by the word "antidepressant." For more than forty years, antidepressant medications have been used to treat problems with panic, as well as a wide range of other conditions. In fact, these drugs work well for panic and anxiety, even when an individual isn't depressed.

Currently, two antidepressants have official approval from the Food and Drug Administration (FDA) for treating panic disorder: sertraline (Zoloft) and paroxetine (Paxil). Although these are the only officially approved drugs, there are a large number of other medications that have been found to be effective. In fact, there is no evidence that sertraline or paroxetine work any better than many of the other products discussed in this chapter.

There are a few things to keep in mind if you are considering antidepressants for your panic disorder. First, these drugs take a few weeks to begin working. However, side effects may appear shortly after starting the medication, and they are often worse during the first few weeks of treatment. It is generally recommended that people continue to take these medications for a year or more before trying to decrease the dosage or discontinue the drug. It is believed the relapse is less likely if discontinuation doesn't occur too early.

SELECTIVE SEROTONIN REUPTAKE INHIBITORS (SSRIS)

The most commonly prescribed antidepressants for panic disorder are the SSRIs. This class of drug works by affecting serotonin levels in the brain (serotonin is a neurotransmitter, which is a chemical that transmits information from one nerve cell to the next). The SSRIs include drugs such as paroxetine (Paxil), sertraline (Zoloft), fluoxetine (Prozac), fluvoxamine (Luvox), citalopram (Celexa), and escitalopram (Lexapro). The side effects of SSRIs vary slightly from drug to drug, but the most common ones include nausea and upset stomach, sexual problems, dizziness, tremor, rash, insomnia, nervousness, fatigue, dry mouth, sweating, and palpitations. In very rare cases, more serious side effects may occur. Starting at a low dosage and increasing the dosage slowly can help to minimize side effects.

Most SSRIs can be discontinued easily. However, some (especially paroxetine) are more difficult to discontinue due to temporary withdrawal symptoms such as insomnia, agitation, tremor, anxiety, nausea, diarrhea, dry mouth, weakness, sweating, and abnormal ejaculation. Discontinuing these medications slowly can help to minimize the symptoms of withdrawal by allowing the person to adjust more gradually to no longer having the medication in the body. The table below provides a summary of the SSRIs and the dosages at which they are typically prescribed.

Selective Serotonin Reuptake Inhibitors (SSRIs)			
Generic Name	Trade Name	Starting Dose	Daily Dosage
Citalopram	Celexa	10 mg	10–60 mg
Escitalopram	Lexapro	10 mg	10–50 mg
Fluoxetine	Prozac	10–20 mg	10–80 mg
Fluvoxamine	Luvox	50 mg	50–300 mg
Paroxetine	Paxil Paxil CR	10 mg 12.5 mg	10–50 mg 25–62.5 mg
Sertraline	Zoloft	50 mg	50–200 mg
Note: Citalopram, escitalopram, fluoxetine, and paroxetine are also available in a liquid form. There is also a new formulation of fluoxetine that can be taken once per week.			
CR = Controlled Release			

OTHER ANTIDEPRESSANTS

The first antidepressant to be studied extensively for panic disorder was imipramine (Tofranil), a tricyclic antidepressant. This drug works on a number of neurotransmitters in the brain, including norepinephrine and serotonin. Another tricyclic antidepressant, called clomipramine (Anafranil), also appears to be effective for treating panic disorder. This medication primarily affects serotonin levels in the brain. Common side effects for tricyclic antidepressants include dry mouth, blurred vision, constipation, racing heart, low blood pressure, sedation, and weight gain. At high doses, clomipramine increases the risk of seizures in people who are prone to this problem. Generally, tricyclic antidepressants are easy to discontinue. They are prescribed less frequently than newer antidepressants, including the SSRIs.

Two newer antidepressants are also showing promise for the treatment of panic disorder. Placebo-controlled studies of venlafaxine (Effexor), a drug that works on both norepinephrine and serotonin, have found this drug to be a useful treatment for panic disorder (Pollack et al. 1996). The most common side effects include nausea, dizziness, dry mouth, and increased blood pressure at higher doses. Mirtazapine (Remeron) is a relatively new antidepressant that also appears to be an effective treatment for panic disorder, based on preliminary studies. One recent study suggests that it works as well as the more established SSRI, fluoxetine (Ribeiro et al. 2001).

A number of other antidepressants may be useful for treating panic disorder, though they are rarely prescribed anymore. For example, phenelzine (Nardil) is a type of antidepressant called a monoamine oxidase inhibiter (MAOI). It reduces panic symptoms, but the side effects tend to be more severe than those of other antidepressants. In addition, MAOIs interact with many other medications, interact with various medical conditions, and require several strict dietary restrictions. Specifically, foods containing tyramine (including certain cheeses, meats, and wines, for example) may not be eaten. Another antidepressant called nefazodone (Serzone) may have antipanic properties, based on uncontrolled studies (in other words, studies that did not include a placebo group). However, this drug should be used with caution due to the potential for liver damage. In fact, this product was recently banned in Canada for this reason.

Not all antidepressants work for panic disorder. For example, Bupropion (Wellbutrin) is effective for reducing depression and for quitting smoking. However, it doesn't seem to do much for panic disorder or other anxiety-based problems.

The table below provides a summary of non-SSRI antidepressants that are useful for treating panic disorder, along with the typical starting dose and daily target dose.

Other Antidepressants Used to Treat Panic Disorder			
Generic Name	Trade Name	Starting Dose	Daily Dosage
Clomipramine	Anafranil	20–50 mg	100–250 mg
Imipramine	Tofranil	10–25 mg	100–250 mg
Mirtazapine	Remeron	15 mg	15–60 mg
Nefazodone	Serzone	100–200 mg	100–600 mg
Phenelzine	Nardil	10–30 mg	45–90 mg
Venlafaxine	Effexor Effexor XR	37.5–75 mg 37.5–75 mg	75–225 mg

Anti-Anxiety Medications

When professionals use the phrase "anti-anxiety medication," they are typically referring to a class of drugs known as the benzodiazepines. These medications include drugs such as alprazolam (Xanax), clonazepam (Klonapin in the USA; Rivotril in Canada), lorazepam (Ativan), diazepam (Valium), and others. Of these, only alprazolam has official FDA approval for treating panic disorder, though there are a number of studies showing that clonazepam is also very effective. Although lorazepam and diazepam have not been studied extensively for the treatment of panic disorder, they have been shown to be effective for other types of anxiety disorders, and lorazepam, in particular, is frequently prescribed for panic disorder, despite a lack of research for this condition. The typical starting dosage for lorazepam is 2 to 3 mg (target dose is between 2 and 6 mg). The usual starting dose for alprazolam and clonazepam is .5 mg per day, with the dosage gradually increasing to between 1 mg and 5 mg per day.

The most common side effects for benzodiazepines include drowsiness, lightheadedness, depression, headache, confusion, dizziness, unsteadiness, insomnia, and nervousness. These drugs should not be taken with alcohol. In addition, benzodiazepines are associated with significant withdrawal symptoms when they are stopped, particularly when they have been taken for an extended period at higher dosages. It is recommended that these drugs be discontinued very gradually, under the supervision of a doctor. Common withdrawal symptoms include panic attacks, anxiety, and insomnia. These symptoms are temporary, and they vary in intensity and duration depending on the drug. Usually, withdrawal symptoms clear up within a few days after the dosage is reduced.

One advantage of the benzodiazepines is that they work quickly (within a few minutes in some cases). Because of that, people sometimes take these drugs on an "as needed" basis, to prevent a panic attack or to stop panic in its tracks. We recommend against using benzodiazepines in this way. Although they may stop your panic attack, they may also set you up to experience withdrawal symptoms a few hours later, perhaps even triggering another panic attack. Benzodiazepines may be useful for individuals who have just begun to take an antidepressant and are waiting for it to begin working, which can take a month or so. One study (Pollack et al. 2003) found that people who took clonazepam (a benzodiazepine) along with paroxetine (an SSRI) experienced greater relief during the first month of treatment than those who took a placebo with their paroxetine. After a few weeks passed, the clonazepam was gradually discontinued because the paroxetine had started working and no additional medications were needed.

Another medication that has shown promise for treating panic disorder is gabapentin (Neurontin). This drug is used mainly for treating seizure disorders, but recent evidence suggests that it may also be useful for treating anxiety and panic as well. In a placebo-controlled trial, gabapentin was no more effective than placebo overall, but when more severe cases were looked at separately, there did appear to be a benefit to using gabapentin over and above the effects of placebo (Pande et al. 2000). More research is needed to establish whether gabapentin is a useful treatment for panic disorder.

Herbal and Natural Remedies

In recent years, natural and herbal remedies have become increasingly popular, but don't believe everything you read about them. Many of these products are marketed for people who experience anxiety and stress, but often there is little to no evidence supporting these claims. There are a few other cautions about herbal medicines. First, in North America they are not regulated in the same way as medications. In fact, they are regulated as nutritional supplements (like foods). Therefore, unlike medications, they don't need to be proven to be effective or safe before they go to market. For many of these products, relatively less is known about their effectiveness, ideal dosages, side effects, interaction effects, and withdrawal symptoms, compared to the other medications discussed in this chapter. Assume that if a product does work, it likely has an effect by altering brain chemistry. Therefore, it probably has side effects, interaction effects, and withdrawal effects, just like other medications.

To the best of our knowledge, the only natural product to be investigated for panic disorder is inositol. This is a variant of glucose (a simple sugar) that occurs naturally in the body and can also be taken in supplement form. Though it's not commonly used for panic disorder, one study found this remedy to be as effective as fluvoxamine, an SSRI (Palatnik, Frolov, Fux, and Benjamin 2001). A number of other products may also be useful, though research is lacking. For example, St. John's Wort appears to be effective for depression (though results vary across studies), and current thinking is that this product shares features with an SSRI. Therefore, it would not be surprising to find that St. John's Wort works for panic disorder as well. However, this is just speculation at this stage; the research remains to be done.

CBT, Medication, or a Combination?

It is difficult to predict in advance who will respond best to CBT versus medication or a combination of these approaches. Some people do best with CBT; others do best with medication, and some benefit most from combined treatment. On average, all three of these approaches are equally likely to be useful.

For some people, combined treatment may work best because the medication helps to give them the courage to do their exposure practices. However, the benefits of combining CBT and medication may only be temporary. For example, in a study combining exposure therapy with medication, one factor that predicted long-term outcome was the beliefs that patients had about what aspect of treatment was most helpful to them. Those who believed that the medication was most important in their recovery were more likely to experience a relapse in their panic symptoms during follow up than those who believed that the exposure made the biggest difference (Başoğlu et al. 1994). In addition, two studies have found that in the long term, medication may interfere with the effects of CBT (Barlow et al. 2001; Marks et al. 1993). One possible explanation is that people who start medication and CBT at the same time respond early to the medication. As they start to feel better, they don't work as hard at their CBT homework, and therefore experience a return of symptoms once they stop taking their medication.

Based on current research, we recommend that most people start with CBT if it is available and affordable to them. If CBT doesn't do the job, adding medication at that point may be useful. Of course, everyone is different. There may be reasons why a different approach is more likely to be useful for you. As we have said over and over in this chapter, any decisions regarding the use of medication should be made in collaboration with your doctor.

Afterword

I f you are reading this section, then you deserve much credit
for getting to this point. Now it's time to take stock of your
progress so far and to develop a plan to maintain and continue the gains you have made. For some of you, this book will
have been enough to have made significant progress in overcoming your panic disorder. For others, this book may have
provided a good start, but you may benefit from additional
readings or from professional help. At the end of this section,
we will cover different options that are available for further
treatment.

Monitoring Your Progress

Over the course of reading this book, you have developed
your understanding of panic and fear. You have monitored
your panic attacks and anxiety and developed skills for replac-
ing your anxious thoughts with more realistic ones. You have
also begun to confront feared situations and physical symptoms and to eliminate safety behaviors. You have learned
about breathing retraining and the importance of reducing
stress, improving your health habits, and maintaining your
relationships. Finally, you have developed a better understanding of the different medication options available for treating
panic disorder.

Now it's time to take a step back, review your progress, and check where you are in relation to the goals you set in chapter 2.

Exercise: Assessing Your Progress

Take some time now to reflect on the progress you have made over the past few months as you worked through this book. Record your responses to the following questions in your journal.

1. Compared to where you were before you began reading this book, what changes have you noticed in terms of the following symptoms:

   - The frequency of your panic attacks

   - Your fear of having panic attacks

   - Your fear of having panic symptoms

   - Your fear that panic symptoms will lead to something bad happening

   - The intensity of your panic attacks

   - Your avoidance of situations

   - Your avoidance of physical symptoms

   - The impact your anxiety has on your work or school functioning

   - The impact your anxiety has on your social life

   - The impact your anxiety has on your ability to carry out day-to-day activities

2. What strategies have you developed?

3. What positive changes have you made in your life?

4. What benefits have come from practicing the techniques in this book?

5. Where are you now in terms of the short-term and long-term goals you set in chapter 2?

6. What are the areas that you need to keep working on?

7. Given the progress you have made, what new short-term and long-term goals do you want to set?

Maintaining Your Gains

Now that you have learned new strategies for managing panic, the next step is to plan how you will maintain your gains. It is important to be prepared for possible increases in anxiety or occasional panic attacks in the future. Occasional anxiety and panic symptoms are to be expected, particularly around times of stress. How you react to the occasional episodes of anxiety and panic are key for determining whether your gains will be maintained or your symptoms will worsen. By being prepared to experience occasional anxiety you will be better equipped to manage it in a helpful way. You now have the basic tools needed to challenge anxious thoughts that may arise or to confront urges for escape and avoidance. You can always refer back to the different chapters in this book to boost your strategies and keep you on track. Remember, your fear of the physical symptoms is what fuels panic disorder. If you view the physical symptoms as just nuisance sensations, they will not have the power to significantly impact your life.

Seeking Professional Help

For some of you, this book may not be enough to completely manage your problems with anxiety and panic. If you have gone through this book but still find that panic is a problem for you, then you may benefit from seeking professional help. There are a number of different professionals who are available to treat panic disorder, including psychologists, psychiatrists, and trained therapists. A good place to start is with your family physician, who will be able to suggest some referrals in your community. You can also use the Internet to find a professional specializing in anxiety treatment by accessing the Web site of the Anxiety Disorders Association of America (www.adaa.org). When selecting a professional, it is important to ensure that they are trained to administer cognitive behavioral therapy or appropriate medication treatments, and that they have experience in treating panic disorder.

Recommended Readings and Videos

Books

Craske, M. G., and D. H. Barlow. 2000. *Mastery of Your Anxiety and Panic, 3d. ed. (client workbook and client workbook for agoraphobia).* Boulder, CO: Graywind Publications, Inc.

Otto, M. W., M. H. Pollack, and D. H. Barlow. 1996. *Stopping Anxiety Medication: Panic Control Therapy for Benzodiazepine Discontinuation (Client Workbook).* Boulder, CO: Graywind Publications, Inc.

Zuercher-White, E. 1999. *Overcoming Panic Disorder and Agoraphobia (Client Manual).* Oakland, CA: New Harbinger Publications.

The first three books in this list are session-by-session workbooks written for clients who are receiving cognitive behavioral therapy for panic disorder with a psychologist, psychiatrist, or other counselor. For each of these, there is also available a session-by-session manual for the therapist. The book by Otto and colleagues is designed specifically for individuals who are taking benzodiazepines (for example, alprazolam) for their panic disorder and are receiving cognitive behavioral therapy in order to discontinue their medications.

Pollard, C. A., and E. Zuercher-White. 2003. *The Agoraphobia Workbook: A Comprehensive Program to End Your Fear of Symptom Attacks.* Oakland, CA: New Harbinger.

This recent book is a workbook designed for individuals who suffer from panic disorder with significant agoraphobia.

Rachman, S., and P. de Silva. 1996. *Panic Disorder: The Facts.* New York: Oxford University Press.

This brief book contains information about the nature and treatment of panic disorder. It is written for the non-professional who is interested in learning more about this problem. It is not, however, a self-help book designed to help an individual to overcome their panic attacks.

Wilson, R. R. 1996. *Don't Panic: Taking Control of Anxiety Attacks.* New York: Harper Perennial.

This is a good book for people who are interested in learning to overcome their panic disorder and agoraphobia, but who prefer not to use some of the larger workbooks mentioned in this list.

Zuercher-White, E. 1997. *An End to Panic: Breakthrough Techniques for Overcoming Panic Disorder, 2d. ed.* Oakland, CA: New Harbinger Publications.

Over the years, this has been the book we recommend most often to our own clients who suffer from panic disorder with or without agoraphobia. It is comprehensive, easy to find, and reasonably priced.

Videos

Clark, D. M. 1998. *Cognitive Therapy for Panic Disorder.* APA Psychotherapy Videotape Series. Washington, DC: American Psychological Association.

This video is produced for professional therapists, but people suffering from panic disorder may also find it useful. The tape shows an entire therapy session with a client who is fearful of having a heart attack during his panic attacks.

Rapee, R. M. 1999. *Fight or Flight? Overcoming Panic and Agoraphobia.* New York: Guilford Publications.

This is an excellent video for those who suffer from panic disorder, their families, and therapists who treat anxiety-related problems. It includes interviews with anxiety experts and people who suffer from panic disorder, as well as demonstrations of most of the therapy techniques described in this book.

References

Abelson, J. L., J. G. Weg, R. M. Nesse, and G. C. Curtis. 2001. Persistent respiratory irregularity in patients with panic disorder. *Biological Psychiatry* 49:588–595.

American Psychiatric Association. 1980. *Diagnostic and Statistical Manual of Mental Disorders,* 3rd ed. Washington, DC: Author.

American Psychiatric Association. 2000. *Diagnostic and Statistical Manual of Mental Disorders,* 4th ed. Text revision. Washington, DC: Author.

Anastasiades, P., D. M. Clark, P. M. Salkovskis, H. Middleton, A. Hackman, M. G. Gelder, and D. W. Johnson. 1990. Psychophysiological responses in panic and stress. *Journal of Psychophysiology* 4:331–338.

Antony, M. M., D. Roth, R. P. Swinson, V. Huta, and G. M. Devins. 1998. Illness intrusiveness in individuals with panic disorder, obsessive compulsive disorder, or social phobia. *Journal of Nervous and Mental Disease* 186: 311–315.

Antony, M. M., and R. P. Swinson. 2000. *Phobic Disorders and Panic in Adults: A Guide to Assessment and Treatment.* Washington, DC: American Psychological Association.

Barlow, D. H., J. M. Gorman, M. K. Shear, and S. W. Woods. 2000. Cognitive-behavioral therapy, imipramine, or their combination for panic disorder: A randomized controlled study. *Journal of the American Medical Association* 283: 2529–2536.

Başoğlu, M., I. M. Marks, C. Kiliç, C. R. Brewin, and R. P. Swinson. 1994. Alprazolam and exposure for panic disorder with agoraphobia attribution of improvement to medication predicts subsequent relapse. *British Journal of Psychiatry* 164:652–659.

Bezchlibnyk-Butler, K. Z., and J. J. Jeffries. 2004. *Clinical Handbook of Psychotropic Drugs*, 14th ed. Seattle, WA: Hogrefe & Huber Publishers.

Broocks, A., B. Bandelow, G. Pekrun, A. George, T. Meyer, U. Bartmann, U. Hillmer-Vogel, and E. Ruether. 1998. Comparison of aerobic exercise, clomipramine, and placebo in the treatment of panic disorder. *American Journal of Psychiatry* 155:603–609.

Brown, T. A., M. M. Antony, and D. H. Barlow. 1995. Diagnostic comorbidity in panic disorder: Effect on treatment outcome and course of comorbid diagnoses following treatment. *Journal of Consulting and Clinical Psychology* 63:408–418.

Carter, M. M., J. Turovsky, and D. H. Barlow. 1994. Interpersonal relationships in panic disorder with agoraphobia: A review of empirical evidence. *Clinical Psychology: Science and Practice* 1:25–34.

Chambless, D. L., and E. J. Gracely. 1989. Fear of fear and the anxiety disorders. *Cognitive Therapy and Research* 13:9-20.

Clark, D. M. 1986. A cognitive approach to panic. *Behaviour Research and Therapy* 24:461–470.

———. 1988. A cognitive model of panic attacks. In *Panic: Psychological Perspectives*, ed. S. Rachman and J. D. Maser, 71–89. Hillsdale, NJ: Lawrence Erlbaum Associates.

Clark, D. M., P. M. Salkovskis, L. G. Öst, E. Breitholtz, K. A. Koehler, B. E. Westling, A. Jeavons, and M. Gelder. 1997. Misinterpretation of body sensations in panic disorder. *Journal of Consulting and Clinical Psychology* 65:203–213.

Craske, M. G., and D. H. Barlow. 2001. Panic disorder and agoraphobia. In *Clinical Handbook of Psychological Disorders,* 3rd. ed., edited by D. H. Barlow 1–59. New York: Guilford Publications.

Davis, M., E. R. Eshelman, and M. McKay. 2000. *The Relaxation and Stress Reduction Workbook*, 5th. ed. Oakland, CA: New Harbinger Publications.

Ehlers, A. 1995. A 1-year prospective study of panic attacks: Clinical course and factors associated with maintenance. *Journal of Abnormal Psychology* 104:164–172.

Ehlers, A., and P. Breuer. 1995. Selective attention to physical threat in subjects with panic attacks and specific phobias. *Journal of Anxiety Disorders* 9:11–31.

Ehlers, A., J. Margraf, S. Davies, and W. T. Roth. 1988. Selective processing of threat cues in subjects with panic attacks. *Cognition and Emotion* 2:201–219.

Febrarro, G. A. R., G. A. Clum, A. A. Roodman, and J. H. Wright. 1999. The limits of bibliotherapy: A study of the differential effectiveness of self-administered interventions in individuals with panic attacks. *Behavior Therapy* 30: 209–222.

Foa, E. B., J. S. Jameson, R. M. Turner, and L. L. Payne. 1980. Massed versus spaced exposure sessions in the treatment of agoraphobia. *Behaviour Research and Therapy* 18: 333–338.

Fuller, M. A., and M. Sajatovic. 2001. *Drug Information for Mental Health*. Hudson, OH: Lexi-Comp.

Goudey, P. 2000. *The Unofficial Guide to Beating Stress*. New York: IDG Books.

Gould, R. A., and G. A. Clum. 1995. Self-help plus minimal therapist contact in the treatment of panic disorder: A replication and extension. *Behavior Therapy* 26:533–546.

Harvey, J. M., J. C. Richards, T. Dziadosz, and A. Swindell. 1993. Misinterpretations of ambiguous stimuli in panic disorder. *Cognitive Therapy and Research* 17:235–248.

Hauri, P., and S. Linde. 1996. *No More Sleepless Nights, Revised Edition*. New York: John Wiley and Sons.

Hecker, J. E., M. C. Losee, B. K. Fritzler, and C. M. Fink. 1996. Self-directed versus therapist-directed cognitive behavioral treatment for panic disorder. *Journal of Anxiety Disorders* 10:253–265.

Hoffart, A., J. Due-Madsen, B. Lande, T. Gude, H. Bille, and S. Torgersen. 1993. Clomipramine in the treatment of agoraphobic inpatients resistant to behavioral therapy. *Journal of Clinical Psychiatry* 54:481–487.

Kenardy, J., and C. B. Taylor. 1999. Expected versus unexpected panic attacks: A naturalistic prospective study. *Journal of Anxiety Disorders* 13:435–445.

Kendler, K. S., M. C. Neale, R. C. Kessler, A. C. Heath, L. J. Eaves. 1992. The genetic epidemiology of phobias in women: The interrelationship of agoraphobia, social phobia, situational phobia, and simple phobia. *Archives of General Psychiatry* 39:273–281.

Kendler, K. S., M. C. Neale, R. C. Kessler, A. C. Heath, and L. J. Eaves. 1993. Panic disorder in women: A population-based study. *Psychological Medicine* 23:397–406.

Kessler R. C., K. A. McGonagle, S. Zhao, C. B. Nelson, M. Hughes, S. Eshleman, H. U. Wittchen, and K. S. Kendler. 1994. Lifetime and 12-month prevalence of DSM-III-R psychiatric disorders in the United States: Results from the National Comorbidity Survey. *Archives of General Psychiatry* 51:8–19.

Lundh, L. G., U. Thulin, S. Czyzykow, and L. G. Öst. 1998. Explicit and implicit memory bias in panic disorder with agoraphobia. *Behaviour Research and Therapy* 35: 1003–1014.

Mannuzza, S., T. F. Chapman, D. F. Klein, and A. J. Fyer. 1994/1995. Familial transmission of panic disorder: Effect of major depression comorbidity. *Anxiety* 1:180–185.

Marks, I. M., R. P. Swinson, M. Başoğlu, K. Kuch, H. Noshirvani, G. O'Sullivan, P. T. Lelliott, M. Kirby, G. McNamee, S. Sengun, and K. Wickwire. 1993. Alprazolam and exposure alone and combined in panic disorder with agoraphobia: A controlled study in London and Toronto. *British Journal of Psychiatry* 162:776–787.

Marks, M. P., M. Başoğlu, T. Alkubaisy, S. Sengün, and I. M. Marks. 1991. Are anxiety symptoms and catastrophic cognitions directly related? *Journal of Anxiety Disorders* 5:247–254.

McNally, R. J., C. D. Hornig, M. W. Otto, and M. H. Pollack. 1997. Selective encoding of threat in panic disorder: Application of a dual priming paradigm. *Behaviour Research and Therapy* 35:543–549.

Moynihan, J. E., and R. N. Gevirtz. 2001. Respiratory and cognitive subtypes of panic: Preliminary validation of Ley's model. *Behavior Modification* 25:555–583.

Munjack, D. J., R. A. Brown, and D. E. McDowell. 1993. Existence of hyperventilation in panic disorder with and without agoraphobia, GAD, and normals: Implications for the cognitive theory of panic. *Journal of Anxiety Disorders* 7:37–48.

Mynors-Wallis, L. M., and M. T. Hegel. 2000. *Problem-Solving Treatment for Primary Care: A Treatment Manual.* Unpublished manuscript.

Norton, G. R., J. Dorward, and B. J. Cox. 1986. Factors associated with panic attacks in nonclinical subjects. *Behavior Therapy* 17:239–252.

Palatnik, A., K. Frolov, M. Fux, and J. Benjamin. 2001. Double-blind, controlled, crossover trial of inositol versus fluvoxamine for the treatment of panic disorder. *Journal of Clinical Psychopharmacology* 21:335–339.

Pande, A. C., M. H. Pollack, J. Crockatt, M. Greiner, G. Chouinard, R. B. Lydiard, C. B. Taylor, S. R. Dager, and T. Shiovitz. 2000. Placebo-controlled study of gabapentin treatment of panic disorder. *Journal of Clinical Psychopharmacology* 20:467–471.

Pollack, M. H., M. W. Otto, S. P. Kaspi, P. G. Hammerness, and J. F. Rosenbaum. 1994. Cognitive behavior therapy for treatment-refractory panic disorder. *Journal of Clinical Psychiatry* 55:200–205.

Pollack, M. H., N. M. Simon, J. J. Worthington, A. L. Doyle, P. Peters, F. Toshkov, and M. W. Otto. 2003. Combined paroxetine and clonazepam treatment strategies compared to paroxetine monotherapy for panic disorder. *Journal of Psychopharmacology* 17:276–282.

Pollack, M. H., J. J. Worthington, M. W. Otto, K. M. Maki, J. W. Smoller, G. G. Manfro, R. Rudolph, and J. F. Rosenbaum. 1996. Venlafaxine for panic disorder: Results from a double-blind placebo-controlled study. *Psychopharmacology Bulletin* 32:667–670.

Rapee, R. M. 1985. A case of panic disorder treated with breathing retraining. *Journal of Behavior Therapy and Experimental Psychiatry* 16:63–65.

Ribeiro, L., J. V. Busnello, M. Kauer-Sant'Anna, M. Madrugo, J. Quevedo, E. A. Busnello, and F. Kapczinski. 2001. Mirtazapine versus fluoxetine in the treatment of panic disorder. *Brazilian Journal of Medical and Biological Research* 34:1303–1307.

Roy-Byrne, P. P., and D. S. Cowley. 2002. Pharmacological treatments for panic disorder, generalized anxiety disorder, specific phobia, and social anxiety disorder. In *A Guide to Treatments that Work,* 2nd. ed., edited by P. E. Nathan and J. M. Gorman, 337–365. New York: Oxford University Press.

Russo, E. 2001. *Handbook of Psychotropic Herbs: A Scientific Analysis of Herbal Remedies for Psychiatric Conditions.* New York: Haworth Press.

Schmidt, N. B., K. Jacquin, and M. J. Telch. 1994. The overprediction of fear and panic in panic disorder. *Behaviour Research and Therapy* 32:701–707.

Schmidt, N. B., K. Woolaway-Bickel, J. Trakowski, H. Santiago, J. Storey, M. Koselka, and J. Cook. 2000. Dismantling cognitive-behavioral treatment for panic disorder: Questioning the utility of breathing retraining. *Journal of Consulting and Clinical Psychology* 68:417–424.

Siegel, L., W. C. Jones, and J. O. Wilson. 1990. Economic and life consequences experienced by a group of individuals with panic disorder. *Journal of Anxiety Disorders* 4:201–211.

Sifton, W. D. ed. 2002. *PDR Drug Guide for Mental Health Professionals*, 1st ed. Montvale, NJ: Thompson Medical Economics.

Taylor, S. 2000. *Understanding and Treating Panic Disorder: Cognitive-Behavioural Approaches*. New York: John Wiley and Sons.

———. 2001. Breathing retraining in the treatment of panic disorder: Efficacy, caveats and indications. *Scandinavian Journal of Behaviour Therapy* 30:49–56.

Taylor, S., W. J. Koch, and R. J. McNally. 1992. How does anxiety sensitivity vary across the anxiety disorders? *Journal of Anxiety Disorders* 6:249–259.

Turgeon, L., A. Marchand, and G. Dupuis. 1998. Clinical features in panic disorder with agoraphobia: A comparison of men and women. *Journal of Anxiety Disorders* 12:539–553.

van der Does, A. J. W., M. M. Antony, A. J. Barsky, and A. Ehlers. 2000. Heartbeat perception in panic disorder: A re-analysis. *Behaviour Research and Therapy* 38:47–62.

Wade, S. L., S. M. Monroe, and L. K. Michelson. 1993. Chronic life stress and treatment outcome in agoraphobia with panic attacks. *American Journal of Psychiatry* 150:1491–1495.

Martin M. Antony, Ph.D., is professor in the Department of Psychiatry and Behavioural Neurosciences at McMaster University in Hamilton, Ontario. He is also chief psychologist and director of the Anxiety Treatment and Research Centre at St. Joseph's Healthcare in Hamilton, Ontario. He has received early career awards from the Society of Clinical Psychology (American Psychological Association), the Canadian Psychological Association, and the Anxiety Disorders Association of America, and is a fellow of the American and Canadian Psychological Associations. He is past president of the Anxiety Disorders Special Interest Group of the Association for Advancement of Behavior Therapy (AABT) and has been program chair for the AABT annual convention. He is actively involved in clinical research in the area of anxiety disorders, teaching and education, and he maintains a clinical practice. His Web site may be found at www.martinantony.com.

Randi McCabe, Ph.D., is chair of the Clinical Behavioural Sciences Programme in the Faculty of Health Sciences and assistant professor in the Department of Psychiatry and Behavioural Neurosciences at McMaster University in Hamilton, Ontario. She is also associate director of the Anxiety Treatment and Research Centre at St. Joseph's Healthcare in Hamilton, Ontario. She is the lead author of *Overcoming Bulimia: A Step-by-Step Cognitive Behavioral Workbook*. She is on the editorial board of *The Clinical Psychologist* and has been assistant chair of the Program Committee for the Association for Advancement of Behavior Therapy (AABT) annual convention. She is actively involved in clinical research, teaching, and education. She also maintains a private practice.

Some Other New Harbinger Titles